Heroes Of The Faith Speak

Seven Monologues

Stephen M. Crotts

CSS Publishing Company, Inc., Lima, Ohio

HEROES OF THE FAITH SPEAK

For more information about CSS Publishing Company resources, visit our website at
www.csspub.com or e-mail us at custserv@csspub.com or call (800) 241-4056.

ISBN 0-7880-1973-2   PRINTED IN U.S.A.

Dedicated to
George Hampton Alley,
my first grandchild.
What will you become in Jesus?

Table Of Contents

And what more should I say? For time would fail me to tell of Gideon, Bar'ak, Samson, Jeph'thah, of David and Samuel and the prophets — who through faith conquered kingdoms, administered justice, obtained promises, shut the mouths of lions, quenched raging fire, escaped the edge of the sword, won strength out of weakness, became mighty in war, put foreign armies to flight. Women received their dead by resurrection. Others were tortured, refusing to accept release, in order to obtain a better resurrection. Others suffered mocking and flogging, and even chains and imprisonment. They were stoned to death, they were sawn in two, they were killed by the sword; they went about in skins of sheep and goats, destitute, persecuted, tormented — of whom the world was not worthy. They wandered in deserts and mountains, and in caves and holes in the ground.

Yet all these, though they were commended for their faith, did not receive what was promised, since God had provided something better so that they would not, apart from us, be made perfect.

Therefore, since we are surrounded by so great a cloud of witnesses, let us also lay aside every weight and the sin that clings so closely, and let us run with perseverance the race that is set before us, looking to Jesus the pioneer and perfecter of our faith, who for the sake of the joy that was set before him endured the cross, disregarding its shame, and has taken his seat at the right hand of the throne of God.

— Hebrews 11:32—12:2 (NRSV)

Introduction

Heroes Of The Faith Speak contains brief biographies of seven such heroes — a forgiving monk in an out-of-the-way land, a gift-giving priest, a teacher at a university, a dirt farmer, a sailor with an idea, a healed shut-in, and a cast-off prisoner. None was great, for only God is great. None did extraordinary things. They, rather, did ordinary things in an extraordinary way. And in Jesus Christ, the world has never been the same.

One may simply read these biographies. Or you may summon up your courage to risk, adopt a modest costume, and portray each character in dramatic monologue. Either way, be inspired by who they were and whom they served.

For, as Hebrews 11-12 says, we are surrounded by a great stadium of history's heroes, who, having run their race of faith, have sat down in heaven's bleachers. From there they cheer us on with our own lives. "You can do it!" "Don't quit. Just a little longer!"

Indeed, they plainly tell us that each of us matters. And we can be the man or woman our world needs in this hour.

Stephen M. Crotts

William Bradford Speaks!

Willa Cather wrote, "The history of every country begins in the heart of a man or woman." And in a very real sense, the United States of America began in the heart of William Bradford of Austerfield, England. He's been called "the first American."

There are those who've argued Captain John Smith was the first American, but after years of exploration he retired to England. Some set forward Virginia Dare, firstborn of the English on American soil, but little is known of her as she was a part of Manteo and "the Lost Colony." Some even clamor for John Winthrop, governor of the Massachusetts Bay Colony, but he only tried to duplicate England in America.

William Bradford was different. No soldier of fortune, he was not an adventurer who came to American shores to get rich quickly, then take the next boat home to Great Britain. Bradford came to stay. He brought his wife. He planned to trade, to build a town, to establish a covenant way community of Jesus Christ.

And stay he did, his colony establishing the pattern for village life that would become the model for hundreds of other towns across North America.

Franklin D. Roosevelt wrote, "Those who have long enjoyed such privileges as we enjoy forget in time that men have died to win them." Such is the case with us here and now, with William Bradford then and there. That's why William Bradford, "the first American," returns today, in this Thanksgiving season, to speak, to remind us, to call us back to the neglected path.

(*At this point the congregation sings the hymn, "We Gather Together." As it is ending, Governor Bradford enters from the rear of the nave, a hoe over his shoulder, giving a series of commands to the Plymouth settlers.*)

John! My good man, take the young men to the shore and dig for mussels and put them in the spring to keep them for our needing.

And a good morning to you, Priscilla! Would you take three of the girls and see that the vegetable gardens are properly weeded?

Samuel, do not be forgetting to fell more trees what for timber for our stockade. Take Thomas with you. As many men as you need. And have Robert finish digging the saw pit.

(Bradford reaches the front of the nave, turns, removes his hat, wipes sweat from his brow, then addresses the congregation.)

You were asking about the sea voyage over. Indeed, we only had one storm. It lasted the entire voyage, September through November, nine weeks! We'd planned to settle south of here, at the mouth of Mr. Henry Hudson's river, but Cape Cod here to the north was where we made landfall, and the none of us had any stomach left for ship's travel. So we settled here.

Ah! This place likes me well! To be sure it's been hard, so many have died, but the good Lord has seen fit for our colony to make a beginning.

So now I've got the hour, and if you like I'll tell you the whole of our story.

If you travel back to England, you'll find my hometown at the southern edge of Yorkshire near Sheffield. My village is Austerfield. Of nearly 200 persons, it is.

Go in the Anglican Church, St. Helen's, and open the baptismal record and it will list my name, "William Bradford baptized into Jesus Christ as an infant, 19 March, 1589."

My father, William, a yeoman farmer, died when I was but sixteen months old. My mother Alice married again when I was four, sending me to live with my grandfather. But after two years he died. I went back to my mother to live, but after a year she, too, died. So at age seven my two uncles, Robert and Thomas, took me in, making me as a family servant.

I was a sickly child unable to do hard work. So I was taught to read and write so as to be useful in recording deeds, making contracts, and such. During this time I read the Bible, also, *Fox's Book of Martyrs.*

When a lad of teenage years, I was shepherd afore the family flocks. And on the hillside there I met another child shepherd, a Christian he was, who began to share the gospel of Christ Jesus with me. Soon I was following him to Babsworth, a village eight miles away, to the church where Richard Clyfton preached. I went every Sunday to learn all I could.

Well, soon my uncles missed me at St. Helen's and forbade me to go to Babsworth. I went anyway, so strong was my love for the Good News.

Gladly, a church was started closer by in Scrooby. And it was there I met William Brewster. He was 41. I was in my early teens. And he quickly became the father I never had. He let me watch him live. He taught me Christ, prayed with me, loaned me books — he was my friend and mentor.

At Scrooby we made a covenant to live together in Jesus Christ. The Bible was our map. In it we found no warrant for bishops, big buildings, traditions, pipe organs, and the likes of Anglicanism. So we met in Brewster's house. He was area postmaster and had a fair-sized house in which we met. John Robinson, a Cambridge College graduate, who could read the Bible in its original languages, became our pastor. And under his eye we became a close family.

But did you know what we were doing in the house church was illegal? The state church of England offered no religious freedom to hold Bible studies outside her walls. And since we were meeting without her approval, when our doings were discovered, five of us were summoned to York to answer to authorities. There we were harassed, threatened, and Brewster's job and house taken away.

This was England in 1607. Queen Elizabeth I was on the throne. There was no law but her. Few could read. There was no public schooling. A family could never own land that was completely theirs. Unemployment was high. Discharged soldiers turned to highway robbery to make a living. There were so many people the government feared a revolt. So there was capital punishment for hundreds of crimes. No trial was necessary. Anyone could be thrown in jail, left to die of disease.

The five of us returned to Scrooby from the church authorities in York. We held a meeting of our covenant and it was decided to quit England for the shores of Holland and her promise of religious freedom. I was seventeen when we set out on foot for Boston, a tiny fishing village on the coast. There were nearly 100 of us who liquidated our holdings, gathered a small bundle, and began the trip.

In Holland we first tried to settle in Amsterdam where there were two free churches. Yet one church's pastor was scandalously involved in sexual misconduct. And the pastor of the second church had no set doctrine and drifted into strange ideas.

So we moved on to Leyden, Holland, a fair city built on thirty islands at the mouth of the Rhyne River. It was a cloth manufacturing center of about 100,000 people. It was also home to a fine university of lively ideas, art, and books. Some say Leyden is the prettiest city in all of Europe!

At first the only jobs we could find were low-paying servants' jobs. But we became Dutch citizens, joined the Guilds, and when my uncles in Austerfield died, I sold my family land, and bought a large house next to the University where our church could gather. I also bought a loom and began to manufacture silk and other cloths.

Now settled, I began to be in want of a wife. Several years earlier I'd met Dorothy May in Amsterdam. She was only eleven years old then, but I never forgot her. And by now she was sixteen and marrying age! I wrote and proposed. She accepted. And we were soon married at my house in Leyden.

By now our church had grown to near 300 souls. We were accustomed to meeting on Thursday nights and twice on Sundays. Our meetings generally lasted four hours each. There was an hour-long opening prayer. Pastor Robinson then read from the Geneva Bible, two to three chapters. A Psalm was sung. Then commenced a two-hour sermon, very meaty and interesting. Next we sang another Psalm, celebrated communion, even a baptism, and closed in prayer.

During this time we came to think of ourselves as God's saints on earth. We were brethren returning to the ancient way of the Bible. We were to come out of the wicked ways of the world and be separate.

How God did bless our twelve years in Leyden! We prospered materially, the church matured, and my Dorothy and I became parents of a fine son whom we named John.

Aye, but there were seeds of trouble sown in Europe. Catholic Spain was at war with Protestant Europe. And it looked like we'd be dragged into it. Some of our children were joining the Dutch Army, falling away from the Covenant. Many of us were becoming more Dutch than English!

Then the idea formed in our minds to make a new start in America: to be free of European wars, to own more land, to live our covenant unmolested, to create a better heritage for our children. We saw ourselves as Abraham, told to move from Ur to the new land God was to show him.

But where? We heard South America was a land of perpetual summer. But the Catholic Spanish were there. Then we got a copy of Captain John Smith's map of Virginia. We saw the northern part of the New World had rivers, natural harbors, forests, and game. Why, Captain Smith himself wrote, "If a man can't make a living there he deserves to starve."

The decision was made to move again, this time to America. We began to sell off our possessions and to negotiate with England for land in the New World. It took several years of hard effort.

The financial backing came from seventy merchant adventurers who put up 7,000 pounds each. (That is nearly a million dollars in today's money.) Lacking ourselves sufficient money to fund the trip, we bound ourselves in labor to these merchants who financed us. Our contract called for seven years' work during which no colonist could earn for himself, only for the merchants. We'd gather lumber, sassafras, and furs, especially beaver skins for fine English hats, ship it all back to England to be sold for the profit of our backers.

About 100 of us in the congregation of 300 agreed to go. Once we were firmly settled we'd call for the rest to join us. Pastor Robinson would stay with the Holland flock and come within a few years. So would our young son John.

The day before we were to leave Leyden, Pastor Robinson called for a day of solemn humiliation before God. A sermon was preached from Ezra 8:21. "Then I proclaimed a fast there, at the river ... that we might humble ourselves before our God, to seek from him a straight way for ourselves, our children, and all our goods." This was followed by a feast in Pastor Robinson's house. Then we wept as we boarded the barges in the river that took us to our ship. I can still remember my wife waving tearfully to our son as we pulled away from Holland's shores.

I wrote of that day in my diary. "So they left that goodly and pleasant city which had been their resting place nearly twelve years; but they knew they were pilgrims, and looked not much on those things, but lift up their eyes to the heavens, their dearest country, and quieted their spirits."

From Leyden we sailed across the English Channel to Southampton, England, where we were to meet Captain Jones and his ship the *Mayflower*. He'd already made several voyages to America, and had been hired by the merchant adventurers to take us over.

We also planned to take a second boat with us, the *Speedwell*. She'd remain with us in America, to be used for trade with the Indians.

By August 5, we were fully provisioned and set out from Southampton for the New World. But trouble hit hard. The *Speedwell* proved slow and leaky. So we had to put in at Dartmouth, England, to try to fix her. After several more weeks' delay, we put to sea once more, only to find the *Speedwell* unseaworthy as ever. So we turned back for England, this time putting in at Plymouth, England. There we had to abandon the *Speedwell*, a bitter blow, for we'd never planned to be self-sufficient as a colony. Rather than farm subsistently, we'd planned to live by trade with the Indians. And the boat was useful to that end.

All of this was too much for many of our brothers and sisters. The loss of the *Speedwell*. Too many fruitless days at sea, seven weeks by now. At Plymouth many of our brethren went ashore determining to return to Holland.

This left us undermanned for the colony. The merchant adventurers panicked and began recruiting anyone off the streets to fill the ranks. We stoutly complained. But what could we do?

So, on September 6, 102 men, women, and children crowded aboard the *Mayflower*. Forty-one of us were covenanted Christians, whilst 61 were strangers to our ways.

Our good ship was 180 tons, not small for her day. She measured 113 feet long, 26 feet wide, was deep-bellied and three-masted. And at a top speed of two miles per hour we set out for the New World, a voyage that was to last 65 days.

The sea journey can only be described as a long beating. Our toilets were slop buckets emptied in the bilge. There was no bathing. No privacy. What little water we had was rationed. Our food was always cold — hard biscuits, salted beef, some beer.

And then came the storm. A continuous tempest of rain, wind, cold, and tossing. We were all seasick. The stench of vomit in our tightly-closed room below decks was awful.

The *Mayflower's* crew, thirty godless sailors, mocked us mercilessly. They threatened to throw our supplies overboard, told us we'd die and be fed to the fishes. One sailor in particular blasphemed our God and taunted us endlessly. He became the only man to die on the voyage over, his body dumped overboard.

Once, a mighty wave crashed over us and broke one of the beams supporting our main mast. It looked like we were done for! But a large press we'd providentially brought along for printing purposes was screwed into place in time to give the sagging beam support.

And all the while we worried over how we could build our covenant way community when the strangers among us so outnumbered the saints. We decided we would lead the colony no matter what!

On Friday, late in the day, November 9 it was, our good ship arrived off the coast at Cape Cod. Then we did fall to our knees and thank God for a safe deliverance.

The next day, a Saturday, we were all anxious to go ashore, but decided it was time to draw the strangers in our midst into agreement with what we'd come to do. So most of Saturday was spent writing out what we called the "Mayflower Compact" and agreeing to our common laws of governance.

Still anxious to go ashore, the next day was Sunday. It being the Lord's day, we obediently rested and worshiped. And come the dawn on Monday we rowed the women ashore to wash clothes whilst the men explored.

We found a water spring, wild berries, and Indians! They peeped at us through the forest, ran from us when we called out. We also found a store of corn and seed the Indians must have hidden. If it hadn't been for this, we'd have starved or had no seed to plant come springtime!

For the next weeks we anchored off Cape Cod on the *Mayflower* whilst Captain Jones, Miles Standish, myself, and others used the small boat to explore the sea. We battled freezing rain, counter winds, hunger, and cold for over a month as we explored for a suitable home for a colony.

Finally, we arrived at the site Captain John Smith had called "Plymouth" on his map of Virginia. It had fresh water, a hill to fortify, a bay deep enough for a ship, and land strangely cleared for agriculture, yet no Indians were to be seen.

We found out later, the Indians who'd cleared the land had been wiped out a year earlier by a plague. Other Indians were afraid to come near, fearful of the plague themselves. So, in God's providence, we'd settled in the only part of the New England coast free from hostile Indians. And the land was cleared already for our crops!

We rowed joyfully back out to the *Mayflower* to bring the ship and the colony ashore. But I was greeted with heavy news. I was told my lovely Dorothy, all of 23, had fallen overboard and drowned, her body never recovered. Oh, the pain! Oh, the loneliness! "Why, God?" I moaned for many a day. Yet, life must go on in a strange and hostile land. And go on we somehow did.

We moored the *Mayflower* in Plymouth harbor. December 18, 1620, it was. Then we rowed the first of the colonists ashore. There was a large rock fortuitously settled at the water's edge which enabled us to step ashore without getting our feet wet. I hear the stone remains to this day, marking the spot we did come to shore.

It being winter in northern climes, we had no time to spare. Our company of nearly 100 persons had no noblemen among us. Only four were past age fifty. We were mostly in our twenties,

18

thirties, and forties. And 33 of us were children! Some of us were coopers, others of us weavers and farmers. And there were carpenters, sailors, soldiers, and tailors among us as well. We commenced to building temporary huts, bringing ashore our supplies, and planning our defense against any possible Indian attacks.

Then the sickness began. The general sickness, we called it. A kind of fever, the coughing of phlegm. In no time two or three of our colony were dying a day. By January and February only six or seven of us were well enough to care for all the rest. January 14 the thatched room of our main storage hut caught fire and we barely managed to save our supplies. All of this, but mercifully the winter of 1620-1621 was one of the mildest on record.

By early spring, of the 102 of us to arrive at Cape Cod, only 56 of us were alive. Nineteen men. The rest women and children. Four entire families were wiped out. Just three married couples remained. Only 21 of us pilgrims survived the first 120 days. Even John Carver, our first governor, died in mid-April. That's when I was elected governor of Plymouth Plantation for the first time.

It was during this dark time God blessed us with another of his providential miracles. March 16 it was. We men were discussing how best to join our meager resources to defend ourselves should Indians attack us. We'd seen them peeping at us from the woods. There had been several skirmishes. And some of our number had gone into the woods not to return. We feared the coming of spring and good weather might bring with it an Indian attack.

That's when, without warning, a redskin, wearing little clothing, walked right into our camp. He had a bow with arrows slung over his shoulders. His hair was cut short, long in the back. He just walked right up to us and said in plain English, "Welcome! You wouldn't happen to have a beer, would you?"

Tall and handsome, the Indian's name was Squanto. He spent the night in our camp; one of us was up all night as a sentry to watch him. The next day he called for his tribe to join us and they sang and danced to entertain us in a most welcoming manner.

It seems Squanto had befriended Captain John Smith years earlier, returned with him to England, learned the language, acquired a taste for English ale, and later sailed home to his native

America. That's when he heard more Englishmen had arrived and he'd come to investigate.

Other Indians visited. We found out their tribe was called Wamponoan, "the people of the dawn," because they were the most eastern tribe. One of their number, Samoset, was very tall and handsome. He became a close friend of mine, the colony not able to survive without him. He taught us the Indian language. He taught us to plant our corn using alewives, or fish, as fertilizer, and to guard it to keep the wolves away. He taught us how to make peace with the surrounding Indians.

The first summer we put our griefs behind us and farmed and built as fast as we could. By fall we had eleven buildings up and a good crop in. We'd learned to fish some, and fowl was easily taken in the woods.

It was then William Brewster recalled October 3 to be a Dutch holiday, a time of thanksgiving for Holland's victory over the Spanish. He encouraged me to declare a similar day of thanksgiving for our good colony and her deliverance through so many perils. So I did so in November.

We were now twenty men, ten women, and the remainder children. We set about gathering wild turkey, shellfish, greens, wine of grapes. And, as it seemed good, we invited our Indian friends so as to strengthen our friendship.

To our horror ninety hungry braves showed up. They did bring five deer with them. But for three days of feasting our ten women had 142 demanding stomachs to fill!

We men played games of skill. Miles Standish, our military leader, entertained our Indian friends with battle drills. And the Indians danced for us.

No sooner was our Thanksgiving celebration over than we heard a ship was coming in. Panic filled our minds! Would it be a Spanish ship out to destroy us? Could it be a French warship that'd rob us and leave us to starve? It turned out to be a British frigate, the *Fortune*, bringing 35 more settlers, but not one box of provisions! And how were we to feed and house these souls when we were barely hanging on ourselves?

Of the new arrivals, most refused to work. They clearly planned to overrun the colony by weight of their numbers, make it their own, and keep us working!

Until now, all our labor was to the common good. All our crops went into the community storehouse, and each of us took out what we needed. Communism, thus, was our way of economy.

Remembering the Apostle Paul's admonition in Thessalonians, "If a man won't work, let him not eat," I as governor ordered our socialist economy ended. I gave each colonist a parcel of land to own, to work as a farm, and the fruits of his labor would be his. Thus ended our crisis of laziness. Though, I might add, some of our number got a mite thin before they learned to labor.

In our early years the good Lord provided for us in so many miraculous ways. When the Indian Squanto grew deathly ill with a fever, his fellow braves gathered to witness his death. We, too, gathered at his bedside, but our intention was to pray for him and nurse him back to health. In his pain, Squanto was very much afraid to die, and he begged us, "Pray for me so I can go to the white man's God in Heaven." Squanto was our first convert.

And another time Massasoit, king of the Indian tribes, became deathly ill. He'd gone blind and was clearly near death. The Indians called for us to come and prayerfully nurse their chief. We did. And again God raised him up, much to the amazement of the Indians.

Another summer, when the colony was up to 180 residents, we experienced a sizzling hot July with no rain. Our crops were drying up. And without a good harvest we'd surely starve come winter. So, we fasted and prayed. And soon God sent a two-week drizzling rain that revived our crops. Again the Indians were most impressed. "When we rain dance, a thundershower comes that washes our crops away. Your prayer brings a gentle rain," they mused.

Though we taught the Indians the gospel, few were converted. They liked our Ten Commandments, all except the one against adultery. "It's not convenient," they said.

As the colony began to take firm root, I began to desire a wife. When the good ship *Swan* put into harbor from England, I learned from the news of home that a lady friend of mine, Alice Southworth, had herself been recently widowed. I decided to write, asking her to marry me. And she agreed, taking passage on the next ship to Plymouth. The day of her arrival I met her at the water's edge in my tattered clothing. We were out of bread, had no ale or meat. All I could set before her was some cool spring water and a freshly boiled lobster. But Alice and I were to be very happily married the rest of our lives.

For your knowing, I remained governor of Plymouth Plantation for most of the first 36 years of its existence. If you study my faith you'll see the burden of it all etched into my countenance. There be so many aches in my heart!

Pastor John Robinson died in Holland, never able to come to America as the Anglicans blocked him. And William Brewster was to die, the man who'd been such a father to me.

The first shipload of lumber and fur we sent for England to help pay our debts was pirated by a French raiding ship. Still, within seven years, the plantation was able to pay off our debts with the merchant adventurers and be completely free.

But ease and prosperity were never completely ours. By now other colonies of England were springing up around us, particularly the Massachusetts Bay Colony and Boston with its Puritans led by John Winthrop. And it grew fast so as to make us an economic backwater.

What prosperity we did achieve seemed to serve as our ruin. For as soon as a young man made money, he'd buy land, move to it, and begin to miss church and grow ignorant of the Lord's ways. Soon there was drunkenness, fornication, and greed in the midst of us. And, discipline as we might, preach as we might, it seemed a flood we could not stem.

Over the years, I carefully wrote a history of our noble covenant ways. It's called *Of Plymouth Plantation*. And the story of every hope, every sorrow is there chronicled for you to read.

I guess you could say I got discouraged with my colony. In my late fifties, I left off writing in my book. Careworn, weary, feeling like maybe we had not fully achieved all we'd set out to do in the Lord, I endlessly mourned.

My good friend Edward Winslow, the colony's ambassador, was in England on business for us. And he decided to resign his post, to remain in Great Britain. One by one all of my friends moved away or died — Standish, Robinson, Brewster, Winslow.

I felt so alone. Except for my Alice and my family and Jesus.

When I'd left Austerfield in England, we were a village of near 200 souls. And now after this toil and suffering, Plymouth was but the same size. And the sins of our lives were still with us. More and more, our youth failed to respect our covenant ways. All they desired was in work and possessions. We were the more eager to improve the quality of our outward estates than we were to perfect our spiritual estates.

I guess I learned the limits of my life. I learned how feeble our spiritual will is, how strong our flesh is. And no matter if one cross the vast ocean, one cannot escape what man is and of our continual need of God's forgiving grace in Jesus.

May 7, 1657, it was. My sixty-eighth year. I'd been ill for some time, taken abed. I'd not slept well the night. Feelings of light and warmth accompanied me. And visions I could not put into words. I awoke strangely refreshed. And I told my wife, "God has given me a pledge of my happiness in another world." I died in Jesus at nine in the evening.

The colony mourned my passing and quietly buried me on the hill overlooking the city. My beloved Alice lived thirteen more years, to age eighty. She, you'll find if you visit the old colony, is buried beside me, our life's work finished. In my history of the colony I concluded, "We have rather noted these things, that you may see the worth of these things and not negligently lose what your fathers have obtained with much hardship."

Ah! But we were once young. We once dreamed dreams and saw visions of God the Lord. But we grew old. And so many of our dreams never came true ...

Ah! But so very many did!

(Bradford exits.)

23

Christopher Columbus Speaks!

Five hundred years ago a man dreamed of reaching the east by sailing west. He sought trade, honor, and souls for Jesus Christ. This is his story.

(*Columbus walks to the front. He is old, somewhat stooped, stiff with arthritis. It is after his fourth and final voyage, a few months prior to his death.*)

Never give up. Never, never, never give up! When God gives you a vision, when his call upon your life is plain, then let nothing deter you. Not wars, nor lack of cooperation, nor money, not your low-born estate, not friends who play you false ... nor even the vastness of the ocean and its endless bounty of the unknown.

My name is Christopher Columbus, son of Susanna and Dominico of the weaver's trade in the fair city of Genoa, Italy.

I made four voyages to the Indies, voyages of discovery. Just over 500 years ago now, it was. And some tell me you want to know my tale. If it be so, then I'm here to provide.

1453, it was. The Muslims captured Constantinople and cut off the only known trade route to the east with all its spices, silks, and other treasures. Though I was but a small child at the time, I remember how hard economic times pressed upon my family. My father often could not get enough wool to weave. So it was that the Mediterranean nations began to explore for a new route to China. And the thinking was that the sea route was safest and certainly lay southward around Africa.

I believed China could be reached by sailing west across the Atlantic. As yet no other seafarer had tried it and succeeded.

In many ways my discovery of America started in 1451 in church at the baptismal font when I was an infant. My parents christened me "Christopher." It means "Christ-bearer." And as I grew to manhood my name became a divine commission.

I do not know the date of my birth. We celebrated our birthdays in that time on the feast day of our patron saint. My parents, in calling me Christopher, were consciously naming me after Saint Christopher, the patron saint of travelers. And his feast day is June 25.

Now Saint Christopher was a giant of a man, a Syrian who lived just after the time of Christ. He was converted to Jesus by a hermit who encouraged him to continue seeking God. "How do I seek him?" the new convert asked. "Fast and pray," the hermit said. "But I don't know how," Christopher complained. "Then be helpful to God's people," the old man encouraged. "Find a river without a bridge and help people cross safely. In time God will reveal himself to you." So it was that Christopher went and found a river without a bridge. There he built a cabin and devoted his life to helping pilgrims cross safely to the other side. And in a life of quiet helpfulness to travelers, Christopher came to know God.

All through my childhood my namesake fired my imagination. Could I live up to Saint Christopher's example? Could I be helpful to people? I used to sit on the wharfs of Genoa and look out on the sea and wonder if I could travel across oceans. I'd even pray I could be the one who'd find a new trade route to the east, perhaps as my name means, bear the name of Christ to people who have never yet heard of his redemption.

My grandfather, Peter Columbus, used to tell my brothers and sister and me the story of Raymond Lull, a missionary to the Muslims in Algeria at Bougee. He'd been stoned and left for dead on the beach by Islamic believers. My grandfather and a fellow merchant happened upon the missionary and, discovering he was not dead, took him aboard their ship. The missionary, as he began to recover, sat up and prophesied. Pointing westward he said, "Beyond this ocean which washes the shores of this continent, there lies another continent which we have never seen and whose natives know nothing of Jesus Christ. Send men there."

Verses like Zechariah 9:10 and Isaiah 51:5 stirred my hankering to sail, to discover, to bear the gospel of Christ. "And he will speak peace to the nations; and his dominion will be from sea to sea, and from the river to the ends of the earth." "The coast lands wait for me, and for my arm they hope."

So it was that I grew up carding wool in my father's weaving shop. But I knew all along I wanted to put to sea, to discover a trade route to the east, to live up to my name and be a missionary. My brother Bartholomew and I used to sail along the coast of Italy in a little boat our father had leased. We'd sell cloth or trade it for wine and cheese. By age fourteen I'd made my first long sea voyage to Chios off Turkey. Then at seventeen, with the economic plight of our family nearing desperation, I signed aboard a trader ship bound for England.

We got caught in a nasty little war and a French ship sank us with her cannon fire. Hurt and frightened, I floundered in the sea, found an oar, and paddled six miles to shore. A fisherman found me and for two weeks nursed my wounds.

As I recovered, I found I was in Portugal near Lisbon where my brother Bartholomew had gone to work as a chart maker. I'd also washed up at the very place where sixty years earlier Prince Henry the navigator had set up a school of exploration.

For the next years I worked with my brother Bart in Lisbon making charts for sea captains and selling books.

There I read Marco Polo's books about his travels to China 200 years earlier and the rich civilization he found flourishing. I read of how the church tried to force him to recant of his fantastic revelations of life in China. His only reply was, "The half of it I haven't told you!"

During these years I continued to make sea voyages as far north as the Arctic Circle and south to the equator. I became a master mariner able to captain any ship, and as knowledgeable of the ocean as any man alive.

Once while walking on the beach near my home, I found washed up on the beach a strange piece of carved wood and exotic plants the likes of which were not to be found in Europe. Surely they had drifted across the sea from some strange land!

That's when the idea began to take shape in my mind: That it was possible to reach the east by sailing west.

Since the time of Ptolemy, educated people knew the earth was round. Oh, ignorant sailors filled with superstitious fears still believed it was flat and if one ventured too far from the sight of land they would fall off the earth. Yet the Bible in Isaiah talks about God "sitting above the circle of the earth." And at Christ's coming, time will be morning in one place, noon at another, and yet night in another! Thus, even holy writ tells us plain the earth is a sphere.

So why not sail to the west to reach China and her rich trade? It'd be out of harm's way from Muslim armies. It'd be shorter than trying to round Africa, and the riches would be fabulous!

I found out other ships had tried it but turned around after a few days. I determined to try for myself. But the ships and crews and supplies I needed were expensive. Only a king could afford it! And here I was, son of a poor cloth merchant, an Italian foreigner living in Portugal. How could I ever meet a king and sell him on my idea?

Week after week I went to church to pray about things. That's when the Lord provided another of his marvelous coincidences! And was she pretty.

As I was strolling home from church with my brother Bart, a young lady dropped her purse and I recovered it for her. Felipa was her name, a high-born lady of Portuguese society. I did like her from the first. And she must have been taken with me, for soon I was called to her house to sell books. I found out her father, a former governor, was now dead. So she lived with her mother and brother. We were allowed to court under the watchful eye of the nuns. I proposed marriage and was accepted. And at age 27, we were wed in the church where we met. A year later our son Diego was born.

Although I was now moderately prosperous as a book vendor and chart maker, I still hankered to put to sea westward on a voyage of discovery. Felipa did her best to talk me out of it. But I'd infected her whole family with my vision! And since my in-laws were well-connected politically, I was able to arrange for an audience with King John of Portugal.

He immediately appointed a committee to study my proposal. While holding me in suspense, King John was secretly trying to reach the Indies by sailing around Africa.

So I waited and waited and waited. Months turned into years. Seven long years. Then in 1485, my thirty-fourth year, both tragedy and rejection struck me like two hard fists. Lovely Felipa took ill and died suddenly, and the King's committee pronounced my plans fantasy. To top it all off, I was nearly broke from the expense of living in and around the royal court.

Seven years of waiting! All for nothing! Widowed. Broke. And not just rejected — my plan was called a foolish fantasy. Oh, in those days I ached to give it up, to quit my vision for the secure life of a prosperous merchant. Yet there was my grandfather's tale of the prophet, my name to be lived up to, and my skill as a seaman. And surely I could never abandon all this and be fulfilled!

So I decided to leave Portugal and try for Spain. With my last money I reached the seaport of Palos in southwestern Spain. Little Diego and I knocked there on the doors of Rabida, a Franciscan monastery. We were given food and lodging. The monks agreed to watch over my five-year-old son and see to his education. And what's more, the monks listened to my vision and were enthusiastic about a voyage west to China and my desire to proclaim Christ. So they introduced me around in influential circles.

That's when I met a rich merchant who was willing to outfit a ship for my westward voyage. But at the last minute he backed out, citing how angry the king might become if he tried it and succeeded without permission.

So I was off to see King Ferdinand and Queen Isabella. I told them of my name and calling, of the vision that burned so brightly in my mind. And the queen was especially touched. She, too, was a Christian with a desire to fulfill the Great Commission to carry the gospel to the world.

Odd, looking back, how alike the queen and I were. We were both born in the same year, both redheads, both Christians, and both focused on missions!

But! It seems as if my life then was a tedious and frustrating procession of "Buts!" But Spain was at war with the Moors, Islamic invaders from Africa. But the war had wiped out the royal treasury. "But, of course, our scientific committee will have to study your proposal for some time." "But if you'll just wait ..."

I was 37 years old by now. And I was spending my whole life waiting!

Months dragged by into years.

I decided to try King John of Portugal again. He was more favorable, but just as he was ready to say, "Yes," Bartholomeu Dias returned from sea, having rounded South Africa to reach China. And it was all off for me in Portugal after that.

So I returned to Spain. My brother Bart wanted me to try France or England for backing, but I decided to wait out Ferdinand and Isabella.

During this time I remarried. Her name was Beatriz, and in a year my second son, Ferdinand, was born.

The Moorish War dragged on and on. Then suddenly, January 2, 1492, it was ended! Spain had won, driving the Muslims from Granada.

The court reconvened, re-studied my proposal, and after a delay of seven years, denied it. "Unrealistic!" they pronounced. "Unfounded." "Imaginary."

Fourteen years gone! Waiting! All to no avail. Wearily I mounted my old swayback horse and, broke, homeless, and in my one tattered coat, decided to try for King Charles of France. It was the lowest point of my 41-year-old life.

Ah! But God works in mysterious ways his will to perform! For the treasurer told the queen of my turn down, told her she was missing a wonderful opportunity with little to lose and much to gain. Whereupon she changed her mind, offering to pawn her royal jewelry if necessary to pay for the expedition. As it turned out, such wasn't called for. The treasury had the $14,000 necessary to fund the voyage west.

So a courier was sent out to find me. I was already out of town but he caught up to me and brought me back to court. There I was commissioned to set forth westward to the spice islands.

I decided to leave from Palos, the seaport west of Spain's Gibraltar. Three caravel sailing ships were put to my use. The *Pinta*, the *Nina*, and the *Gallega*, which I renamed *Santa Maria* or *Holy Mary*. A merchant who owed the king a favor had to put up his ships.

Ninety men soon signed up, outfitting and provisioning the vessels. We painted three huge red crosses on each sail. Then on August 3, 1492, in my forty-first year, the crew met in the church of St. George in Palos to pray. The king and queen themselves were there to pray Godspeed to us. And I gave command, "Weigh anchor and proceed in the name of Jesus!"

We sailed southwest to the Canary Islands. There was a known steady westward wind available from those shores, also a last chance to take on water and food.

But near the Canary Islands the *Pinta's* rudder slipped its hinges, I think a deliberate attempt by her owner to put the ship out of commission so as not to risk her on the voyage. Reaching the Canaries, repairs took three weeks.

While we were waiting in the Islands, a huge volcano erupted, belching out fire and illuminating the nighttime sky. My crew was afraid, seeing it as a bad omen. I told them it was only God Almighty showing us his power, a power that was for us, not against us.

Come September 6, repairs made, we weighed anchor and sailed west from the Canaries into uncharted western seas. For the next thirty days we held to a due west compass bearing. All the while I estimated our speed and position by dead reckoning.

The men were restless, afraid we'd come too far to make it back. I had to do my best to coax them on day after day.

At sunrise we gathered on deck to sing God's praises. I purposely forged a duplicate ship's log that grossly under-calculated the distance we'd sailed. When a head wind beat against us, a wind that nicely would have taken us home, it required all my skills to persuade the sailors to persist in our voyage westward.

Then came the day we sailed into the Sargasso Sea, "the sea of weeds." Right in the middle of the Atlantic! As far as the eye could see! The ocean was covered with seaweed! And there we were becalmed. The men were petrified. "Surely our ships will become bound fast and we'll starve!" I had to promise a rich reward if we sailed on.

October 7, 1492. A full thirty days at sea. No sight of land. The sailors were restless. Mutiny was in their minds. Then the shout,

31

"Land, ho!" But to our bitterest disappointment, it turned out to be a cloud band low on the horizon.

It was at this point I had to strike a bargain with the crew. "Give me three more days. Just three days. If we do not make landfall in 72 hours, we'll go home."

Here again God was gracious. The *Nina* found a flower adrift in the sea. A sailor retrieved from the water a piece of wood with iron fastened to it. Then we saw a flock of birds. I quickly abandoned my compass heading west and sailed in the direction the birds took. That night, October 11, about 10:00, I thought I saw a light flickering on the horizon. Other sailors agreed. Then at 2:00 in the morning, October 12, clearly in the moonlight, an island appeared. Trees, surf pounded on a sandy shore. Land! This time it was no mistake!

Bedlam broke out on board. We raised our flags, fired our cannons, and sang hymns of praise. After 33 uncertain days at sea, we'd finally reached the Indies!

Come first light we moved closer to shore to investigate. That's when we first saw the Indians! Stark naked! Every one of them!

I donned my best clothes, a green coat and red cape, and, with the Christian flag unfurled, led the shore party in. There I fell on my knees and thanked God for his mercies. And we claimed the land for Jesus and for Spain!

Looking back, I realize now how easy it would have been for the Muslims to have discovered America first and made it Islamic. And another mercy! Where we came ashore the Indians were friendly. The Taino Indians as it turned out. It could have been otherwise. The nearby Caribs were cannibals. And the Aztecs on the mainland practiced human sacrifice. But we were spared.

The natives, Indians we called them, watched us from a safe distance at first. But we befriended them with gifts. They particularly liked our beaded necklaces and caps. Soon these strange people were swimming out to our ships.

Now the Indians were handsome, with painted bodies and short dark hair. We quickly noticed some had gold earrings in their noses. Soon we were introduced to smoking tobacco, parrots, cotton cloth, exotic fruits, and something called the hammock, which natives sleep in as it is strung between two trees.

I called the island we found San Salvador, meaning "The Savior." But since it was small, and clearly not the mainland of China or Japan, we followed the Indians' directions and sailed southwest for the land the natives called "Cuba."

Island after island passed by until we reached a huge land mass with fresh flowing rivers. That's when I realized our fastest ship, the *Pinta*, had sailed off and left us. Martin Pinzon, the captain, had proven me false and, overcome with gold fever, had abandoned me to seek his own ends!

There was nothing to be done but to go on. So for many days we investigated the shores of Cuba. Still finding no great Indian cities of trade, we sailed eastward reaching another land mass which so reminded me of Spain I christened it "Hispaniola." Today it is known as the island of Haiti and Santa Domingo. There on December 24, 1492, after ten weeks of exploration of the Indies, disaster struck! In the night a storm wind caused the *Santa Maria* to slip anchor and flounder on a reef. She stuck fast, and we had to abandon her on Christmas Day.

Safely ashore, but with only one ship to take us home, I decided to build a colony. "Navidad" or "Christmas" I named it. Thirty-nine crewmen agreed to settle it. And salvage from the *Santa Maria* would stake them until we returned on a second voyage.

So it was on January 2, 1493, I boarded the tiny *Nina* with my crew, said my good-byes, and sailed for home. No sooner had we reached open seas than we spotted a sail. Turned out to be the *Pinta* with her scalawag of a captain Pinzon who just happened upon us. And together, with a favorable east wind, we made for Spain.

After thirty days at sea, a horrible storm struck. For a full fifteen days Satan did everything he could to sink us before we could report our discovery. I so despaired of reaching Spain that I wrote down the details of my journey, sealed it in a bottle, and tossed it into the sea in hopes someone would learn of our fate. And we prayed to our God for deliverance.

That's when the storm began to lessen, and within a few days we found ourselves in the Azores Island group. The officials were amazed at us. Said they didn't know how we had survived. Said it was the worst storm they had ever seen.

It was March 15, 1493, that we returned again to Palos, Spain. For 32 weeks we'd been gone. A voyage of 224 days. I, myself, was ever so glad to be home. At 42 years of age, an older man in those days, I was moving slowly, stiff with arthritis.

And, oh, my! The sudden acclaim we received! I rode horseback across Spain to where Ferdinand and Isabella were in court. I was received as "Admiral of the Ocean Seas," made governor of all I'd reached, and asked to make a second voyage as soon as I could be outfitted.

In all, I made four voyages to the Indies. I could tell you of many adventures and sorrows. Adventures of crossing the Atlantic in 21 days, of the colony at Navidad being destroyed by Carib Indians, of a hurricane wiping out the later colony of Isabella, of how I explored South America, the Mosquito Coast of Central America, and the island, Puerto Rico. I could tell you how worms ate my ships on the fourth voyage, and how I spent a year and five days marooned on Jamaica. I could tell you of the joy of sailing with my sons Diego and Ferdinand.

Seems I was a good explorer but a poor administrator. Many in Spain, along with those who sailed with me, were smitten with gold fever. And the new colonies I brought them to were not making them rich quickly enough. Many wanted to quit for home. They derided me as "Admiral of Mosquitoes" and during my third voyage a newly-appointed jealous governor of the Isabella Colony had me put in chains and sent home in disgrace!

Here in Spain I've found my patron Queen Isabella has died, and King Ferdinand has lost interest in me. Most of the royal court finds me tiresome, and all the promises of financial reward are forgotten. I am worn out, arthritic, and for the most part, bedridden. Death will claim me in a few months in a modest house in Valladolid, May 20, 1506. I am but 53 years old.

Though I clung my whole life to the belief I had sailed to China, I remained confused as to where I had arrived. And it was a frustration to me and my countrymen that we could not find the rich spice countries of trade.

Looking back with the wisdom of 500 years of hindsight, I cannot honestly call what I did the discovery of the continents of North and South America. After all, the Indians were already there. Further, the Norwegian Leif Eriksson and the Irish monk Brenaden were all in America before me.

What I did was encounter the New World and give a report of it to Europe. Times were such that my findings were recognized and acted upon. Thus the sea path between Europe and America was officially opened and commerce begun.

My life also serves to illustrate the two natures of man. Indeed I nobly sailed west to live up to my name — Christ-bearer! It was my heart's desire to evangelize the Indians. And from 1492 to 1820 Spain alone sent 15,000 missionaries to the New World establishing missions from South America to Saint Augustine in Florida to the far west in California.

But the base, sinful nature of our humanity also reared its ugly head. Gold fever and greed led to wholesale slaughter, rapes, and pillage of many Indians across America.

Yet, in all this, God was sovereign. The Indians gave Europe corn, tomatoes, rubber trees, tobacco, rice, and venereal disease. The Europeans gave the Indians Jesus Christ, horses, and fatal smallpox. In fact, over the next 200 years the majority of Indians were wiped out by European fevers. So, in the interchange between the new and old world, history-changing forces none of them could either imagine or control were at work.

Hardly eleven years after my death, Martin Luther was to begin the Protestant Reformation. And in the warring convulsions that resulted, many Christians saw the New World so underpopulated, as a place to plant their new Christian communities. Scarcely 100 years after my discoveries, Puritans, Quakers, and Catholics were founding settlements built on Christian values. Certainly only a sovereign God could manage such a feat that would give rise to the United States and her constitutional example of freedom and the incredible vitality she has shared with the world in education, missions, free enterprise economy, and more.

At my birth, my countrymen believed the best lay behind us. We looked to the past to discover our greatness. Hence, there was little interest in the future, in science, in education, or Christian reform.

Our flag had as its motto, "No more beyond!" But after my voyages the "No," was dropped and our motto affirmed, "More beyond!"

As I leave, thanking you for hearing my tale, I challenge you with your own future. For certainly there is always more! More beyond!

As I had, may you have a good name, seek a vision from God, and though you suffer privation, setback, and endless waiting, if you but trust in God and persist, you will surely plant his flag on new territory. Never give up! Never, never, never give up! Though all men fail you, though you be poor, lowborn, and though your sea be vast and the wind against you, yet God is faithful.

(*Columbus exits.*)

(Originally published in *Long Time Coming!*, CSS Publishing Company, 2001.)

Martin Luther Speaks!

On July 6, 1415, Prague preacher John Huss was led to the stake to be burned as a heretic. Huss was condemned for preaching the gospel, for calling for a return to the biblical faith, for cleansing a corrupt priesthood. The Council of Constance meeting on the Swiss border stripped him of his priestly vestments, a sooty chain was fastened around his neck, and just before the flames burned him, he, making a pun of his last name, Hus, which means "goose," said, "Today you are roasting a lean goose, but hardly 100 years will have passed and from these ashes shall rise a swan who will preach the gospel more fairly than I. And no net of yours will snare him, no trap capture him." Huss died singing. Just to the northwest of Prague, exactly 102 years later, Martin Luther began the Protestant Reformation.

(*The sound of Gregorian chant is heard. Suddenly, the peaceful music is interrupted by the sound of several hammer blows. Martin Luther enters dressed as a doctor, carrying a Bible.*)

Big doors swing on the smallest of hinges. And my life became the hinge on which the Reformation swung. Bethlehem, Nazareth, Israel — all nowhere places. Yet they were the hinges of history giving us Jesus, the Christ. Wittenberg, Germany, I, Martin Luther (*bows*), the doorway to the Castle Church — all nowhere places, and a simple monk, yes, a modest man, yet they've become the hinge on which great things swing.

I must admit, I'm still a bit bewildered. All I did was nail 95 theses — debate points — on the door of Castle Church. And from there a chain of events was loosed that led to the Protestant Church. Like the woodpecker pecking on a tree when suddenly a bolt of lightning struck, splitting the tree in halves, the woodpecker got up, shook his feathers, and said, "God, I didn't know I had it in me!" Indeed, I didn't have it in me. But Christ did. And in his providence he gave his gospel of grace to the world.

The church of my day had lost the gospel of Jesus. What few Bibles there were belonged to the great cathedrals, they were written in Latin, and chained to the lectern. Only two percent of people could read. And those desiring to read scripture had to have the bishop's permission to do so.

Everywhere superstition abounded. Illiterate churchgoers said their rosaries while priests communed with God at the altar. In Germany there were said to be the relics of enough apostles to make up eighteen men. And a greedy church soaked the people selling church offices, indulgences, and a glimpse of the true cross along with other dubious relics.

Priests were sexually immoral, bishops were vainglorious, and at one time in the late 1300s, there was not one pope, but three, all hurling excommunications at one another. Germany was tired of the confusion, tired of being drained financially, tired of feeling insecure over salvation. All this and much more had transpired over the years to kindle in people a desire for renewal, for true knowledge, for an awakening.

In 1298 A.D., Marco Polo, returned from his travels to the Far East, published a book, much copied and eagerly read, detailing his marvelous exploits. The church asked him to recant of his fantasies. "Lies," they called them. "Behold the half of it I haven't told you," was his only reply.

Besetting disasters were to come heavy upon Europe. In 1347 the Black Death swept the continents from India to Iceland, killing entire monasteries, wiping out villages, half of city populations. And in the early thirteenth century the devil's own horsemen led by Genghis Kahn terrified us from the steppes of China to the gates of Prague, as unstoppable as a plague of locusts. Then came the Muslims. In the Middle Ages they took Jerusalem, then North Africa, Spain, and on into southern France. Indeed, these things fell heavy upon us.

Ah! But God was at work. Just nine years after my birth, Christopher Columbus encountered a whole new world. Johan Guttenberg of Germany perfected a movable type printing press. Great universities were beginning to tutor larger numbers of students. And the middle class was born. So many had died of war and plague that a workers' shortage resulted. This meant able-bodied laborers could demand more pay, and as they prospered, they could afford to move about, to gain an education, and to think for themselves.

I, Martin Luther, was born to a miner and his wife in Eiselben of Saxony in Germany. At great sacrifice my parents educated me, intending their son to become a lawyer and care for them in old age.

I schooled at Erfurt University. A bachelor's degree was followed by a master's and eventually a doctorate — which my hat signifies. Two things were to happen in my studies to shape me in important ways.

One: ours was a death-stalked culture. Growing up, several of my brothers and sisters died of the plague. And a teacher, a friend of mine at the university, was murdered by a disgruntled student with an ax. His death terrified me. What if it had been me? Would I have gone to heaven or hell? I did not know.

The second event was a thunderstorm. I was returning one day to school when the sky blackened and suddenly a lightning bolt knocked me to the ground. "Saint Anne," I cried in prayer, "save me and I will become a monk!"

True to my word, and much to my father's dismay, I presented myself to the Augustinian cloister in Erfurt and devoted myself to God. I was a good monk, too. Desiring to please God and earn forgiveness of my sins, I applied myself to endless fasting, confessing of sins, singing of Psalms, and sleeping without a blanket in winter. Once I traveled to Rome on business for my order. There I climbed the Lateran steps, kissing the place where Christ fell. The pope had assured Catholicism that such a pilgrimage all but assured one of salvation. But all I could think when I finished was, "Who can say I did enough? That my works are good enough to merit heaven?"

I began to hate God. The prize of salvation seemed so out of reach for a sinful man like myself. My anxiety over my sins, my fear of God's judgment, and my terror at dying and being cast into hell left me exhausted.

This is when my pastor, the Reverend Johann Von Staupitz, suggested I divert my monkish energies and self-strivings to teaching at a newly-opened university in Wittenberg, Germany, a walled town of 2,500 people with just as many students. He dispatched me to the Augustinian monastery there, and for the first time in my life I began to study systematically the Bible and prepare my lectures.

My office was in the tower. There I poured over the Psalms, the book of Romans, and Galatians. I came to see the Bible was alive. It has a voice that speaks to me. It has feet and it chases me. It has hands that grasp me. And it was in these studies that Jesus Christ laid his claim on my life. Romans 1:17 was especially difficult for me: "The just shall live by faith."

Let me explain. The word "religion" is a Latin word. *Re* means "again." *Legio* means "to bind." Hence, religion is to bind back.

Now all religions agree on two facts: 1) We once had a close relationship with God. 2) We lost it in sin. Where religions disagree is on how that relationship is restored.

Most religions are active religions. Man must do something to earn God's love — behave, pray, give alms, self-denial. Yet I came to understand that Christianity was not an active religion, but a reactive religion.

The gospel teaches that our relationship with God is so hopelessly broken that we could never fix it ourselves. So God, in his love, repaired it for us in Jesus Christ who died in our place on the cross, who rose again, and now offers us salvation as a gift to be received by faith.

When I was a child I climbed a tree and, looking down from my perch, grew frightened. I surely didn't want to go any higher. But when I looked down I became dizzy with heights and clung to the tree, screaming in terror. That's when my father came to the base of the tree, held out his big strong arms, and soothed, "Jump, Martin! I'm here. I'll catch you!" I fell safely into his arms. Reading the Bible I came to see my sinful plight the same. I was up a tree in sin. Not wanting to go on, yet I could not climb down by myself. So I was helpless. That's when Jesus came to me saying,

"Trust me, Martin. Let go of your sins. Fall into my arms. I will save you."

So it was I came to understand salvation was a gift to be received, not a prize to be won. I saw the gate of heaven opened and by faith in Christ I stepped through.

About now, my new faith was sorely tested. A Bishop needed to pay for his office, and the pope of Rome needed more money to build his new Vatican church. So they issued a sale of indulgences. Johan Tetzel, the priest, came into a near region with his flamboyant preaching, "When a coin in the coffer rings, a soul from purgatory springs!" I was incensed. How could the church so brazenly preach something so contradictory to the Bible? That's when in my thirty-fourth year of life I nailed the 95 theses on the door of the castle church. October 31, 1517, Halloween, the eve of All Saints' Day when Christians talk of death, heaven, and our security with Christ.

Now you need to know colleges are always debating something or another, and we used the cathedral door as a bulletin board. It was there I simply served notice that there were 95 points of disagreement I had with the church. And I wished to argue them from the Bible to see if the church was right or wrong.

When the printing press published my list, it was as if I'd struck a match in the dry tender of medieval discontent. Soon all of Europe was discussing my issues. And over the next several years I was maligned by the pope as a "drunken monk with a quarrel" and hauled before civil and ecclesiastical courts in Heidelberg, Augsburg, Leipzig, and Worms. The pope called me "a wild boar loose in the Lord's vineyard" and excommunicated me, also ordering that my books be burned. I, in turn, burned his excommunication bull along with a number of unbiblical Catholic writings. This I did in Wittenberg in 1520 at the city gate. There was no going back now! As we say in German, "The bear is loose!"

When I was proclaimed an outlaw of church and state, Emperor Charles V called me to the city of Worms on the Rhine River in western Germany. There I was to give an account of my discoveries from reading the Bible. My friends begged me not to go. I would be arrested and put to death, they feared, like John Huss. But God's Spirit bade me go! And to my comfort 100 German knights and my prince, Frederick the Wise, vouchsafed my protection.

A crowd of over 2,000 rejoicing people met me as I entered the city. I, a simple monk, brought to stand before emperor, cardinals, bishops, and princes for the hope of the gospel! Expecting to debate, I was silenced, scolded, and told to recant or face death. Asking for a day to think it over, I came back the next day, and in a small voice said, "I cannot recant. My conscience is bound to the Word of God. And unless I can be proved wrong from scripture, here I stand. I can do no other. God help me. Amen!"

The church gave me a running head start before they'd seek to arrest me for execution. But Prince Frederick kidnapped me to the castle in Wartburg. And there I grew a beard and carried a sword, calling myself Knight George. In my ten months of hiding out I managed to write sermons, tracts, even books arguing my biblical views. The Lord even gave me grace to translate the New Testament from Greek to German in but eleven weeks. All of these were printed and read by an ever-widening and eager public. Thus I was doing battle with Satan using pen and ink and paper — and the Word of God!

Meanwhile in Wittenberg the pot of reformation was boiling over. My good friend Philip Melenthon seemed helpless in his leadership. Professor Carlstadt offered full communion, said mass in German, priests married, monks and nuns quit the cloister, and students rioted, smashing icons and statues. Pastor Thomas Munizer even voiced the violent overthrow of civil order by the peasants.

I had to return. I had to risk my life by coming home to take control of matters before the gospel was discredited by lawlessness. So, with Saxon nobles protecting me, I returned to live out my life in Wittenberg, doing battle with the devil with sermons and prayer, with discipleship and love. All from God's Word.

Over the next decades my life was a bustle of work. In 1534, we published the entire Bible in German. Why, the translation was so good Moses seemed more German than Jewish!

I wrote *Three Treatises*, and then my best work, *The Bondage of the Will*, along with countless tracts and sermons.

In 1527 while struggling with a long bout of depression, I took a German beer-drinking tune, paraphrased the words of Psalm 46, and created the hymn, "A Mighty Fortress Is Our God!"

You ask about my personal life. At the age of 41, I took a wife. It happened in the most amazing way! Twelve nuns asked me to help them quit the covenant for the Protestant faith. I arranged for a fishmonger to smuggle them out in empty pickled herring barrels. Three of them returned home. I found husbands for eight others. But for the twelfth lady I came up empty time and again. She was 26, red of hair, and named Katherine Von Bora. My father said I should wed and sire children to ensure a heritage. I began to see it as a way to set an example of the freedom scripture gives priests to marry. And it also seemed a good way further to spite the pope. I told Katie that while I did not love her I could certainly learn to do so in Christ. And so we wed. You can imagine my surprise waking the next morning with pigtails on my pillow.

And ours was a happy household. I wouldn't trade my Katherine for all the wealth of Venice. Six children were our issue over the years. As the Prince gave us the old monastery to live in, our household bustled with children, guests, and students. We punctuated the table talk with my lute playing, the singing of Psalms and hymns! Christmas, when the snow lay on the ground and we celebrated God's gift of Jesus, was my favorite. Coming home from a Christmas Eve service, I spied an evergreen tree ice-icicled and aglow in the moonlight. It was so lovely I cut it down, hauled it by the fireside, and decorated it with candles for Jesus' birthday. Looking back, that was the first Christmas tree, a Yule tradition Germans brought with them worldwide. I also wrote for my children a carol lullaby, "Away In A Manger." Ah, it is an earlier heaven to have a wife, a family. What a contentment to rock a baby's cradle while writing a sermon!

Yes, indeed! But there were hardships. The uprising of the peasants led to a bloody civil war costing thousands of lives. The Reformation splintered into a thicket of unholy confused congregations. And my list of ailments multiplied like pimples — hemorrhoids, diarrhea, gout, obesity, depression, constipation, insomnia, dizziness, ulcers on my leg, kidney stones, and a maddening ringing in my ears.

About now, some of us Protestant leaders undertook to visit the reformed churches of Saxony. To our great despair we found them to be in a sorry state — ignorant pastors, corruption, sin, and bad doctrine. Out of our visit came a push for better schooling, the greater use of hymnody to teach sound doctrine, and I wrote an easily remembered catechism as a means to teach the Bible to all people. We even developed the Augsburg Confession to help ministers to stay within the boundaries of biblical thought. In 1517, I said, "No," to the people and "Yes," to Jesus. Now in 1530 the people were joining me in saying, "Yes," to the gospel.

In living as a reformer, I learned firsthand that criticism is the easiest part of any job. It is far easier to criticize the church and walk off than it is to put something better in its place.

Sometimes I despaired at the foolishness I saw all about me. I once went on strike in the pulpit, refusing to preach. The students were so unruly, so ... vile and incorrigible, I told Katherine to pack up, we were leaving. But farewell to all those who want an entirely purified church. Theirs is plainly wanting no church at all.

My consolation came in visiting a dying youth. When I asked him, "What will you take with you to God?" The boy said, "Everything that is good." "But," I pressed, "how can you, a poor sinner, bring anything good to God?" The youth said to me, "I take a penitent heart sprinkled clean by Jesus' blood." When he said this, I knew the gospel I had labored to preach was doing its work all over Europe. My heart swelled with joy, and I told the youth, "Then go, dear son. You will be a welcome guest to God."

In my later life, my daughter Magdalena died of sickness as I held her in my arms. I wept over her grave. With all my troubles as an outlaw, with all my health struggles, and the stress of leading the church, I told Kate one day, "I am sick of this world. And it is sick of me."

In my sixty-second year, while traveling with my three sons attempting to settle a dispute among Christians, I fell ill at Eiselben. Severe chest pains and other miseries beset me. At 2 a.m. on February 18, 1546, I uttered my last words, "We are beggars, it is true." Then I died safe in the arms of Jesus.

I'm buried beneath the pulpit of Castle Church in Wittenberg. And today in Worms where I stood firm in the faith of Christ, there is a statue of me holding a Bible in one hand while pointing to it with the other. The inscription reads, "If it be God's work, it will endure. If man's, it will perish."

Today, Lutheran Christians stand as a testament to the gospel of Jesus Christ. It is the largest Protestant denomination in the world. Through Protestant faith the gospel has circled the globe with churches, universities, hospitals, missionaries, art, music, and justice. And the world is the better for it.

(Strains of J. S. Bach's "A Mighty Fortress Is Our God" begin to rise.)

But ours is an unfinished work. For this life therefore is not righteousness, but growth in righteousness; not health, but healing; not being, but becoming; not rest, but exercise. We are not yet what we shall be, but we are growing toward it. The process is not yet finished, but it is going on. This is not the end, but it is the road. All does not yet gleam in glory, but all is being purified.

(As Luther says his last line, he exits through the central aisle.)

Saint Patrick Speaks!

At one time nearly 100 years ago the nation of Ireland suffered a severe potato blight. Famine killed hundreds of thousands of people. And many millions of Irishmen emigrated to the United States. These colorful people brought with them March 17, Saint Patrick's Day. Who is this Patrick? When did he live? What was his life? Today, by special arrangement, we have Patrick with us to tell his own story. But before he comes, a little Irish music to get you in the mood.

(*A tape of Irish music is played. After two minutes, Patrick himself enters to walk up the center aisle.*)

Welcome! Welcome, my friends! The Lord is with you!

By the stars of Killarney, if you ain't a handsome lot! Top o' the morning to ya!

Permit me to introduce myself. My name is Sucant, it is! Except I changed me name to Patrick. But then I be getting ahead of meself.

I've come to tell you me story, I have. A tale of privilege, of slavery, of trial and adventure, grace and forgiveness. It's a story guaranteed to bring a smile to yer face, a tear to yer eye, and faith in yer heart.

Born I was in 389 A.D., near the English border ... close to Dunbarton, not far from the Severn Estuary. Me father was a wealthy farmer, Mum a homemaker. Father's name was Calpurnius. Aye! And a mature Christian he was, elected a deacon in our local church.

Yes, ours were a Christian home. I can shut me eyes and recall to mind the love between me parents. I remember grace at supper, home-cooked meals, church services three and four times a week, farm chores, sunsets, rosy cheeks, and warm beds. Looking back, it's sad I took it all for granted. I thought everyone lived like that. I

47

even thought being a Christian was something you were born with — like red hair or blue eyes.

When I were sixteen, alarm spread across the coast land: "The pirates are back!" The worst sort of brigands, they were. And on another raid! Mostly they stole chickens and lambs. But there be some rape and murder as well.

This time they came to my farm and they stole me! One minute I was hiding out in the haystack, the next I was bound, kicking and screaming, and thrown into the hold of a ship. Crossed the Irish Sea, we did. And there they did sell me off as a slave to an Irish chieftain in Mayo near Antrim.

Aye, a slave I was for six fretful years! A shepherd mostly.

At that time the Irish were a pagan lot. Druids by religion. Superstitious. Fearful. Thirsty for blood. Why, fighting were the way of life for the Irish. Whiskey was their sacrament. Their neighbors' blood their entertainment.

No sooner had I arrived than I was ordered to bring six lambs to the Ulster chieftain's tribal banquet. A raiding party had just returned victorious and the male lot was feasting success. The poor captured rival chief was bound in a wicker basket and roasted alive over an open fire. All these years have passed and I can still hear his shrieks of pain. It haunts me whole life.

I sat behind a tree shivering in terror, crying me eyes out. A soldier punched me and glowered, "Take care and be a good servant, laddie, and see such do not be happening to you now."

For six years I lived in such misery. Six long years. Lonely I was. Big tormented. And I clung to the faith me parents had taught me. The belief of Jesus Christ, the Savior of sinners, hope of the lost. I said 100 prayers by day and almost as many by night.

An interesting thing, suffering. It can make you or break you. Why, put a potato and an egg in a pot o' boiling water and the potato will grow soft, the egg will hard boil. Put persons into suffering and some will grow hard whilst others will soften. In my pot of boiling sufferings I grew soft in God's hands. I grew teachable, eager to hear his words, faithful, caring. I tell you, those six years, pain-filled as they were, they be the making of me.

A poet said:

A tree that never had to fight for air and sun and light,
That stood out in the open plain and always got its share
of rain,
Never became a forest king, but lived and died a grubby
thing.
A man who never had to toil with mind or hand 'mid
life's turmoil,
Who never had to earn his share of sky and light and
air,
Never became a manly man, but lived and died as he
began.
Good timber does not grow with ease —
The stronger the wind, the tougher the trees,
The farther the sky, the greater the length,
The rougher the storms, the stronger and the greater
the strength.
Through winds, fears, rough seas, and snows,
In trees, as man, good timber grows.

Aye, many a mortal owes the grandeur of his life to his sufferings. For the Bible says, "Suffering doth produce endurance, and endurance — character, and character — hope" (Romans 5:3).

Spring it was, of my twenty-second year, my sixth in captivity, that I made good my escape. In the night God gave me a dream. He told me to go to a shore where a ship would be waiting for me. I did! And it was! I crossed the Irish Sea again, and returned to my home. For months I wrestled to put the ugly past behind me mind, to forget Ireland ever existed. But the terror, the butchery, life treated so cheaply — it bound me tight as a fist.

I traveled to Gaul, present day France, and off Cannes in the Mediterranean Sea, joined the island monastery of Lerins. After some years I moved to Auxerre where Saint Germanus mentored me in the faith.

If you go taking a magnet and a piece o' iron and rub themselves together, you be having two of the same magnets. And that's how Christian disciples be made. Jesus rubbed up against Peter. Paul, his Timothy. And Germanus, me. Through the gospel, he tutored me how to forgive my Irish tormentors, how to start a new life.

Such progress I made that in 417 A.D., at the age of 28, I was ordained a deacon. The word "deacon" from the Greek being *diaconos* or "slave." Transformed from the slave o' the Irish Druids to the slave o' Jesus Christ I was!

At my ordination I shucked off me Anglo name Sucant and took the Christian name Patrick, meaning "fatherly." Such was my new life — new friends, new town, new name, new service.

About then, while meditating in scripture, I, Patrick, had a vision of God the Lord Christ. The Irish pagans were in misery beckoning to me. "We beseech you to come and walk among us once more."

I was thunderstruck! Me? Return to the Irish lowlifes who'd enslaved me, robbed me of my youth, spoiled some of the best years of my life? How could I ever forgive the bums, love them, walk among them again? Why, my life belonged here in Gaul in the quiet serenity of the monastery!

Many months waking and sleeping I wrestled with the call. It was my own Garden of Gethsemane. Then came the day I knelt as Jesus before God and prayed, "Nevertheless, not my will, but thy will be done." I would journey to Ireland, cross the Irish Sea again as a slave — the slave of Jesus Christ! I would offer the Ulstermen the gospel.

Actually, I began to be excited as the mission took hold of me. In France there be many Christians. What with a church in every village it were hard to find a being who'd not heard the gospel. And the Spirit kept whispering in my heart, "Why should these people hear the gospel again and again when the Irish haven't even heard it once?"

If you be aworking picking grapes in the vineyard on the front row where there's many a worker and the grapes be few and the workers bicker among themselves and shove one another to get at the few grapes, but on the second row and third row of the vineyard there be few if any pickers, yet many grapes ripe for the picking, wouldn't it make good sense to leave for the back rows? So I began to see Ireland as the unpicked grapes of the good Lord's vineyard. And I was to go there and harvest the fruit.

When I shared my vision with the brothers and sisters of the church, they were immediately perturbed. One: I, Patrick, was an uneducated man. If you read my testimony, called *Confessions*, which I wrote when I were 61, you see it be wrote in crude Latin. I guess it'd muster a "C" in one of your schoolboy grammar classes. So the elders worried about sending a poorly-educated man such as I to the mission field.

A second concern the elders had was with the Irish themselves. Never before had the gospel been taken outside the Greek- and the Latin-speaking world. The Irish spoke the Gallic language. How could one learn it? Could the Bible be translated? Could anyone relate to Druid pagans? A missionary would likely be killed. And such would be a waste of time and life.

For fourteen years I remained in the monastery of Auxerre praying, fasting, studying, sharing the vision for Ireland. I took comfort in Paul's conversion and it being full fourteen years of quiet preparation before he ventured forth on his first mission journey. God, you see, is a very patient and thorough preparer. He will first build you, then he will take you to where you may build others.

Came the welcome day the church was set to try for Ireland. Palladius was to be the leader, me the assistant. But whilst we be packing, Palladius took ill and perished. So, suddenly I was in charge. Me the backup, the unlettered man. But we must carve our lives from the wood we're given. So I journeyed west to Ireland alone. The year was 432 A.D. I was a 42-year-old man.

Disembarking from my ship, I went straight to the Irish chieftain at Tara, King Laoghaire. And to him I boldly spoke, "The way you're living is not how life's supposed to be. Are you happy in your drinking, killing, and thievery? These Druid gods cannot give life meaning. I tell you, there's no hope in yer Stonehenges, in yer rites of butchery. It's but a religion of fear, of spells and witchery that leads to despair! I offer you good news! I offer you your Creator! You be made in his image, after his likeness good. But sin has eaten yer heart up and left you cold, ruthless, and unfit. So God has come to us personally in Christ Jesus. 'This is who I am,' God says. 'This is what I'm like, what I want!' Then Jesus sacrificed himself for our sins on the cross. But God raised him from the dead proving neither sin nor death is stronger than God's love. Now he invites you to come to him and be made over, forgiven fer all yer trespasses, to lead a life of love."

Do you know what happened? King Laoghaire ran me off with snarled curses. And his Druid priests mounted a determined resistance with every spell and curse of their demon charm books! Suddenly, I was very thankful for those fourteen years of thorough preparation, for being schooled in spiritual warfare. In Isaiah God promises, "No weapons formed against you shall prosper." 1 John teaches, "He who be in you is greater than he who is in this world, the Devil himself." And Ephesians 6 warns us to armor up so as to be able to stand against the Devil. I had sewn for me this tunic in the shape of a shield or breastplate. And inside it I wrote out my confidence in the Lord so to cover my heart from evil.

"I bind unto myself today the strong name of Trinity ... I bind this day to me forever, by the power of faith, Christ's incarnation ... Christ be with me, Christ within me, Christ behind me, Christ before me ..."

After prayer and fasting forty days on a mountain, I trudged back to King Laoghaire. He was drunk at a banquet. The candles flickered dimly, and a tiny sparrow flew in from the night, flitted about, and made his escape out of another window. Red-eyed and weary, Laoghaire stood and said, "My life is like that sparrow. I flew in from the dark of who knows where, I circle the banquet hall of life, snare a crumb or two of bread, and shall leave in death to go who knows where? Whence? Wither? Why?" he moaned.

I rose to preach the gospel. And this time the king wanted to learn more. Many hours of discussion took place over the next weeks. And Laoghaire was close to believing, but he was having trouble understanding the Trinity. "How can God be one person yet three, Father, Son, and Spirit?" I explained the matter time and again, yet the king's head was as thick as a turtle's hide! Finally, in exasperation, I plucked a shamrock. "How many plants do I have here?" "One," the king said. "But it has three leaves — the Father, the Son, and Holy Spirit!" I exclaimed. And the king understood. And he believed and was baptized.

My good friend Laoghaire began to travel with me as I proclaimed Christ in Ulster. He'd stand beside me to give moral support as I preached. Now, I, Patrick used to emphasize my sermon points by stamping my shepherd's crock whilst I labored with words. And once I accidentally drove it through the meat of Laoghaire's foot. He winced in pain, but never cried out, thinkin' he was that it was all a part of the Christian ritual.

Some of ya be wondering why I dress as I do. Ya see, the Irish could not read. So I had to show them a picture.

My long shirt of Irish linen is the sort all Ireland wore, a reminder that Christ became one of us. My tunic in the shape of a shield or breastplate is a reminder of the protection God gives us from all evil.

This staff? I was once a shepherd slave tending sheep. Now I am the servant of Christ tending his flocks of people.

This hat so like a crown? I wore it to remind the Irish there was reward in serving the Lord. The Holy Book says God gives crowns in heaven to those who win souls, who pastor, suffer, look to his return, and keep themselves pure.

And what of this green stole I wear about me neck? Aye! Ireland's a beautiful land. It be twenty shades of green every direction a person look. But there's more to this yoke than green! For if you but look you'll see it has the look of serpents all entwined in Trinity.

The Druid Satan worshipers charmed a poisonous snake to bite and kill me and Laoghaire. And when one tried, I killed it! And like Jesus in Mark the fifth chapter who cast the demons into swine and then drowned them in the sea, I cast the Druid demons into the snakes of Ireland and they slithered into the sea to drown! That's why there are no snakes in Ireland even to this day!

Back in France many prayers were offered for our Irish mission. And the Lord gave grace to the Irish people so that many believed.

We bound the converts into communities of monastic churches. Little villages of quiet work, common meals, Bible study, and disciplined faith. 1 Thessalonians 1 tells of Paul, Timothy, and Silas living the faith before the Greeks and how the Thessalonians began to copy their lifestyle. This is what we did in our churches, we modeled in our behavior Christ's love. People watched us, liked what they saw, and wanted in from the Druid cold.

The church became the place we taught reading and Bible. There we gave the people the education I never quite had. In the book of Ecclesiastes it is said, if a sword is dull, you have to exert more strength. But with a sharp sword a man succeeds more easily. So knowledge helps a man succeed.

For the next 31 years I set about sharpening the Irish Christian converts so they could succeed. I did preach to them, organize them into monastic churches, and give them a vision to help others. I was Christ's magnet. They were my iron.

We built a cathedral to worship Christ in Armagh of Ulster. It was my administrative center. And a fine place it was!

Sad, but in the 1,600 years that separate my life from today there isn't much physical evidence left of my life. I never married. I have no descendants. There's not even a marked grave over my remains. And in the 1600s Oliver Cromwell's Puritan reformers burned my cathedrals and monasteries. All's left I built is a four-sided bell I used to call the faithful to worship, a stone chair at the Rock of Cashel, and my *Confessions*, along with a letter I wrote to a soldier.

Sometimes I get distressed about these things. It's only natural for us to want to leave our mark on the world. You're thinking it's a pity with so little to show for 72 years of life. But think again! I have no grave, to be sure! But neither does Jesus or Moses or David or Paul! I have no wife, but then in Christ, I am in the marriage of all eternity! And I have no descendants. Yet the Irish be my children!

Aye! I remember it well. March 17, 461 A.D., it was. My seventy-second year. I died and was carried by angels to heaven.

It's said I, Patrick, was the apostle to the Irish, that when I came I found Ireland all pagan. But when I left, I left it all Christian. 'Tis true. I baptized over 120,000 people into the faith and founded over 300 churches. And for the 200 years after my death, educated Irish missionaries left Ireland to carry the gospel across the known world.

My friends, if you want to leave yer mark on the world, don't write it in stone or steel and glass. Write it on the hearts of people. Offer them Jesus Christ! "For the world passes away and the lust thereof, but he that doeth the will of the Lord abideth forever."

A man came up to me recently. An attorney. Fifty-three years old. Rich. But bored with his life, looking for more, wanting to put something back. He asked if he could come to Ireland with me and help in the work. I told him, "Go find your own Ireland!" For there's aplenty of towns and neighborhoods, families and nations needing to be harvested for Christ. And if you but listen, God will call you to your part of his vineyard.

Another man said to me, "Patrick, I want to be just like you!" But I said, "One's enough of anyone I ever met. Be yourself! When you stand before the Lord, he won't ask you why you weren't me or Moses or Paul. He'll ask you why you weren't you!"

Yes, I'm Patrick. A Welshman. Once enslaved against my will. Scarred by torture. Uneducated. Single. Childless. The church's second choice for the mission. A late starter for Ireland at 42. But Jesus Christ plus Patrick was enough. And Jesus Christ plus you shall be enough as well.

I told you me story was certain to bring a smile to yer lips, a tear to yer eyes. But what about faith to yer heart? Have you received Jesus as your Savior? It's easy enough. You but turn from yerself and sin to Jesus, believe in him, receive his spirit, and live to obey him. Then be finding your way to a good church for encouragement and a real education. From there God'll show you your vineyard.

So ... I must be a leaving ya now. But afore I do, I've a blessing to you.

May the road rise to meet you,
May the wind be always at your back,
May the sun shine warm upon your face,
The rains fall soft upon your fields,
And, until we meet again,
May God hold you in the palm of his hand.

(*Saint Patrick exits.*)

Saint Nicholas Speaks!

(Saint Nicholas, in his vestments, proceeds in to the beautiful taped fanfare of a Christmas song. He stops at a microphone, sits on a stool behind a small lectern, and soberly intones ...*)*

> *You'd better watch out! You'd better not cry!*
> *You'd better not pout, I'm telling you why:*
> *Santa Claus is coming to town.*
>
> *He knows when you are sleeping,*
> *He knows when you're awake,*
> *He knows when you've been bad or good,*
> *So be good for goodness sake!*
>
> *He's making a list, checking it twice,*
> *Gonna find out who's naughty or nice,*
> *Santa Claus is coming to town.*
>
> (J. Fred Coots and Haven Gillespie, 1934)

Ho! Ho! Ho! I just love what you people write about me! Just listen to this ...

> *Down the chimney St. Nicholas came with a bound:*
> *He was dressed all in fur from his head to his foot,*
> *And his clothes were all tarnished with ashes and soot;*
> *A bundle of toys he had flung on his back,*
> *And he looked like a peddler just opening his pack.*
> *His eyes, how they twinkled! His dimples, how merry!*
> *His cheeks were like roses, his nose like a cherry,*
> *His droll little mouth was drawn up like a bow,*
> *And the beard on his chin was as white as the snow.*
> *The stump of his pipe he held tight in his teeth,*
> *And the smoke, it encircled his head like a wreath.*

He had a broad face and a round little belly,
That shook when he laughed like a bowl full of jelly.
(Clement C. Moore, 1822)

Isn't that a hoot!

And I really love the song, "I saw Mommy kissing Santa Claus, underneath the mistletoe last night!"

All this is wonderful! And I'm flattered! But it's really not me. No, I'm not omniscient. I don't know if you're bad or good. I have no way of knowing if you're sleeping. And I'm not omnipresent. I can't be everywhere at once on the same night.

Only God can be these things.

I also don't live at the North Pole and drive a sleigh with eight tiny reindeer.

Who am I then?

In one of your newspapers I saw a cartoon. A man reading the newspaper was saying to his wife, "Honey, it says here that scientists have discovered the true meaning of Christmas!" I guess you could say I did that 1,700 years ago!

My name is Nicholas.

I was born in 270 A.D., in the seacoast town of Patara in Asia Minor. That's in the present day country of Turkey.

My mother and father were wealthy, and they raised me in a Christian home. Sadly, they died in a plague when I was a little boy.

As I grew older I traveled often and got into the habit of using my money to help people. When I was nearly fifty years of age I took a trip to the Holy Land. I wanted to see Galilee, Jerusalem, Bethlehem — the places where Jesus walked! During that journey God spoke to my heart and I determined to go home and become a pastor in the church. In the Lord, this seemed the best way for me to really help people.

So I returned to a village near my birthplace, a town called Myra. The time was around 320 A.D. My job was to be the bishop or pastor of Christians in the area.

Now, in those days we dressed like this. Today I've noticed your doctors wear green, nurses often wear a white uniform, and your football players wear such odd attire — big padded jerseys with numbers on them, knickers, and funny hats! I dressed this way to remind people who Jesus Christ is. My red bishop's coat is a reminder of the blood of Christ that cleanses from all sin. (*Cross yourself beatifically.*) The Lord be praised! My hat is called a miter. It is a symbol of Christ as the helmet of salvation. This stole is a symbol of the yoke of Jesus, a simple reminder we are all his servants. And this staff is a symbol of Jesus, the Good Shepherd, and how I care for his flock. And these shoes? Why, they are to keep my feet warm!

So, who am I really? I am Nicholas of Myra, Turkey. I lived 1,700 years ago. And I was the pastor of the church of our Lord Jesus Christ.

In my day it was dangerous to be a Christian. Rome ruled our world. And Diocletian was the emperor. Aye! And he was such a pagan. He made himself a god and ordered everyone to burn incense to his image, to bow before him, and to chant, "Diocletian is lord!"

I refused and I taught my people that only Jesus is Lord. So the emperor rough-handled me. He persecuted my people and exiled me, and forced me to live away from my flock.

Then, God be praised! (*Cross yourself.*) Mean old Diocletian died and was replaced by Constantine as emperor! And he was a Christian. He allowed me to return to Myra and my parish. What joy! What a feast! What worship there was in the church when we met together in God's house! Freedom! I was able to spend the rest of my life with my people!

For 22 years I watched over my church. And during this time I grew especially fond of children. You see, I was single. My parents were dead. So, my family became the church. And others' children became as my own in the faith. How I loved to sit a little child on my lap and tell him the stories of Jesus!

One of my other joys was gift giving. Jesus said, "It is more blessed to give than to receive." (*Cross yourself.*) The Lord be praised!

Once a man in my church went bankrupt and was going to have to sell his three beautiful daughters into slavery, a practice quite common in those days. When I heard about it, I prayed to God Almighty, our provider, collected an offering, and in the dead of night stole past the man's house and threw a bag of gold into an open window.

Well, it seems the little girls had left their freshly-washed stockings by the chimney to dry and, don't you know, that bag of gold landed in a sock! Imagine everyone's surprise the next morning when they were dressing and they found enough money to pay off their debts and keep the family together.

Another time a young lady wanted to marry, but she had no dowry. Hearing of her plight, I gathered some money, climbed on her roof in the black of night, and dropped some gold coins down her chimney. Wouldn't you know it! They fell into her stockings hung to dry by her chimney with care! The next day she found the money, and a wedding was announced right away! Imagine their joy! And because the gift was given in secret, there was no one to thank but God!

And do you know what else? I hear tell that on Christmas night people still hang their stockings by the fireplace in hopes that something good will fall into them by morning!

I, Nicholas, was not just a minister with a soul for children and gift giving in secret. I was also a scholar.

The church in my day was having trouble deciding what to believe about Jesus and the Bible and the Holy Spirit. So Emperor Constantine called the church leaders to meet in Nicea, Turkey, in 325 A.D. There we canonized the Bible. We decided which books were to be included and which were to be left out. We also summed up our beliefs in the Nicean Creed:

> *I believe in one God, the Father Almighty, maker of heaven and earth, and of all things visible and invisible: and in one Lord Jesus Christ, the only begotten Son of God, begotten of his Father before all worlds, God of God, Light of Light, Very God of Very God, begotten not made, being of one substance with the Father, by whom all things were made; who for us men and for our salvation came down from heaven ...*

Lest you think that I, Nicholas, was perfect, let me hasten to confess I was a sinner, too. Once at the Council of Nicea, I so violently disagreed over a point of theology with another pastor that I punched him in the jaw. And, for shame! I was arrested on assault charges and spent the night in jail.

I'm sorry I did it. Such behavior is not Christ's way. Our Lord said, "Go the second mile. Turn the other cheek." (*Cross yourself.*) The Lord's name be praised!

So, for 22 years I was an elder to my people — teaching, evangelizing, offering communion, baptizing, burying the dead, and performing weddings. But all the while, my favorite chores were always the children and gift-giving in secret.

Jesus called me home in 342 A.D., on December 6. By then I was well-known in the area. And many Christians had begun to follow my example in Christ and have ministries of their own. It became popular to hold a feast and worship service in my memory on December 6. Why, people would dress up like me, hold children on their laps, and often give them gifts.

Some began to say I was a saint. In 1087, a group of Italian businessmen dug up my bones in Myra and reburied my remains in Bari, Italy. There I am enshrined in the church of San Nichola this very day.

And in the 1980s, the Pope, in an ecumenical gesture of good will, gave some of my bones to a Greek Orthodox church in Flushing, New York.

My! My! How things get out of hand. Soon my memory began to overshadow people's devotion to Jesus. The nations of Greece, Russia, and Sicily made me their patron saint. Merchants, bakers, seamen, children, and especially virgin girls looking for husbands began to look to me for help.

Certain cities in Holland, Switzerland, Germany, Austria, and Italy made me their town patron.

What is a patron saint? Today many of your young lads collect baseball cards that have sports heroes like Barry Bonds or Sammy Sosa. You might say a patron saint is someone's favorite Christian hero who becomes an example to follow.

Well, all of this went on and on. Churches named after me, little pictures of me hung around their necks, people even began to pray to me as if I were God!

Thank God for the Reformation that began in Germany in 1531 with Martin Luther and his insistence that Christians use the Bible as a guide for their faith! You see, I was never meant to become more popular than Jesus. Things had clearly gotten out of hand.

The Protestants, the Puritans, made it illegal to mention my name. During the 1600s it was forbidden to light a candle, exchange gifts, sing a carol, or make a mincemeat pie. Christmas, it was decided, was to be celebrated at home, quietly, soberly.

But people will celebrate! And if we don't teach them how to sing and feast and dance and make merry before the Lord, then the world will. So, because the church unwisely banned my name, the world took over and secularized my memory.

In England, I became Father Christmas. In France, I was called Papa Noel. In Russia, I became Father Frost. But in Holland Christians were stubborn. And they refused to forget the life I lived in Jesus Christ.

The Dutch pronounced my name Saint Nicholas as "Saint Niclaus" or Santa Claus.

The first Dutch ships to sail to the New World in America had my figure carved on the bow of their ships. This was true of Henry Hudson, the great explorer, as well. The first church building built in New York City was named after me. It's still there in Manhattan to this very day.

When the British took New York from the Dutch my memory began to fade. Americans thought of me as the English did. I was Father Christmas. And they soon began to make up stories about me that weren't true.

In the 1820s a dentist named Clement Moore wrote a poem for his sick child to cheer her up. It was called *'Twas The Night Before Christmas*, and in it children were told I lived at the North Pole, drove a sleigh pulled by eight reindeer, and that I was fat!

Actually my nickname was "Skinny." You see, as a follower of Jesus I often fasted, often controlled myself so as to serve God more effectively. And God made me a tall, slender man.

In 1863, during the American Civil War, Thomas Nast drew a cartoon picture of me for *Harper's Weekly* magazine. He, too, pictured me as plump. He gave me a long white beard, rosy cheeks, and dressed me in red with a sack of toys slung over my back.

Well, as you can see, some of their ideas about me are true, some are not.

All this for over 100 years now, and you can see how cloudy my memory has become.

I'm not from the North Pole. My home is in Turkey! I don't have little elves to help me. I worked with deacons and elders. I don't know who has been bad or good. I'm not making a list and checking it twice. And I could never fit down your chimney.

Today, there are many who love Santa Claus so much they forget Jesus. And there are others like the Puritans of old who hate me. Why, a church nearby burned me in effigy! All of these extremes are too much! It's better to remember the real Nicholas. I was a Christian who lived 1,700 years ago. I loved God's people, especially children. And I gave gifts in secret.

I just today overheard a Christian complaining, "Look what the world has come to!" No! I say, No! Look who's come to the world! He complained, "Just look what the world has done to Christ's birthday!" Again, No! No! It is far better to look at what Christ's birth has done to the world.

He has made people like me, old Nicholas!

I once asked a child, "What is a saint of God?" The little girl, thinking of the heroes of the faith who are pictured in stained-glass windows, said, "A saint is someone who lets the light in." That's what I, Bishop Nicholas, Santa Claus of Myra in Turkey, want to be for you. I am one of the great cloud of witnesses that stands to encourage you on as you run your own great race of faith.

I want to point you to Jesus Christ who saved me, who gave me children to love, who gave me a generous heart and a place to serve. I want to point you to the God who became one of us that we might become one of his. And I want to point you to your own town as a place to serve.

I see there are children here who need to be told stories, gifts that need to be given in secret. And just as I did, so can you.

Stand with me, now, please, and together let us join our voices in a hymn of praise to Jesus, the Christ. (*Cross yourself.*) Praise be to God!

> *O come, all ye faithful,*
> *Joyful and triumphant,*
> *O come ye, O come ye to Bethlehem.*
> *Come and adore him ...*

(*After the song, the people sit down. Nicholas opens a sack and offers gifts to all: candy, a special Christmas ornament, frankincense, perhaps myrrh.*)

(Originally published in *Saint Nicholas Speaks* by CSS Publishing Company, 1991.)

Paul Speaks!

His name is Saul, Hebrew meaning "loaned." He was named after an earlier Saul, the first king of Israel. But while King Saul was tall physically, our Saul is short. At his baptism someone nicknamed him "Paul," which is Latin for "shorty." But though he is short physically, he stands tall spiritually.

From Tarsus, a port city in present-day southeastern Turkey, Paul was Jewish, a maker of tents and sails. But on the Damascus road Jesus met him in a blinding conversion, and Paul was never the same.

Today we meet Paul in prison. After three effective mission journeys, Paul was arrested under false accusations by Jewish and Roman authorities and confined to a jail cell where he has languished for several years now.

He refers to himself as "an ambassador in chains" and busies himself writing letters, encouraging his visitors, and talking to his guards about Jesus Christ.

(*Lights come up on Paul who is wearing a long shirt and cloak, with a chain on his wrist. He speaks to an unseen guard.*)

Lunch break over, Cornelius? I'm still here! Yes, your favorite prisoner!

Look, I need a favor, Cornelius. My friends from Ephesus are here. They need to talk about my letter to their church. Will you unchain me? You can trust this face! (*Paul holds out his wrists and the chains are released.*)

The Lord bless you, my son! (*Lowers voice.*) Whether you want it or not!

Oh, and another thing, Cornelius! Just a tiny favor. May I borrow your armor?

No, I'm not planning to make war on Rome.

Yes, I can remember I'm the prisoner and you're the man in charge.

It's just that I used you as a sermon illustration and I need your gear to explain how things are to my friends. Yes, I was flattering.

Thank you, Cornelius! Thank you. May the Lord bless you and bring your stubborn heart to the faith of his blessed son, Jesus the Christ! And come the day we call our sons Paul and our dogs Nero!

Uh? Don't push it, you say, Cornelius. Okay. Sure.

(*Turns to his Ephesian visitors.*)

Now we're ready! Pull up some dust and have a seat.

You were saying you've read my letter and you understand most of it.

Let's see. I made three points. One: Christ is seated with God in heavenly places and we share his glory. Two: God has bestowed upon us his Holy Spirit and we should walk in him. Three: We must take our stand with Christ against Satan in this evil day.

Oh, I see. It is the last point you're having trouble with. Look at the final paragraph of my epistle. There are four points: We are at war. Satan is our wily foe. We can stand our ground against him. And we have been given effective armor to wear in the battle.

Here, let me show you what I mean.

Gird With Truth

Lo, these many months I've suffered in prison. Cornelius and the other soldiers, many not so kind as he, have guarded me. I am chained to them daily. Without a shred of privacy we eat, bathe, sleep, and even dress watching one another.

That's when it hit me! A soldier's armor! It is an illustration of our protection in Christ!

Just look! (*Takes off his cloak.*) This is my long shirt. It's loose fitting to my feet. We wear it for protection from the sun. It's cool in summer, warm in winter. But it's hard to run in, much less fight!

So, a soldier going into battle would tie up his skirts and fasten them with a belt at the waist. His sword and breastplate would hook into this belt and not flop around. Thus the soldier could maneuver.

When Jesus washed the disciples' feet, he girded his loins like this to be free to stoop, to work without hindrance.

My young friends, in serving the Lord it is vital we strip down to the truth, that we unclutter our lives. The world around us is so like a long shirt twisting around our ankles. All our trips and games, our money-making schemes and endless worries keep us from maneuvering spiritually. Jesus said, "No one can serve two masters, God and mammon." It's like trying to ride two horses at once. It can't be done!

So we must strip down to the essentials and gain perfect freedom of movement.

A student of the Greek masters recently confessed his education to be a total waste of time. "It gave me spokes but no hub, knowledge but no meaning, information but no values. I am lost, totally clueless as to my purpose in life," he said.

The scriptures can help us find that meaning, those values, the hub of life. Scripture is truth. Jesus said he is "the way, the truth, and the life." And we are to gather our lives up in this truth. As the Psalmist wrote, God "desires truth in the inward parts." And deep down, we in Christ know the mystery of marriage, of the second coming, and our glorious future with Christ in heaven!

Breastplate Of Righteousness

After girding his loins, a Roman soldier dons his breastplate. I call this the breastplate of righteousness. (*Puts it on.*)

This means Christians do not only know the truth in our loins, we follow it. The young Christians of the church in Antioch used to say, "Don't talk the talk if you don't walk the walk!" We must hear and obey, learn and do.

When Alexander the Great invaded this part of the world in 333 B.C., he caught one of his soldiers drunk and disorderly. "Soldier, what is your name?" he fumed. The soldier slurred, "My name isss Dalexander." Shocked at having his own name associated with such unsoldierly conduct, the great conqueror yelled, "Young man, either change your name or change your behavior!"

Righteous behavior is like a breastplate. The physical armor protects our vital organs from sword thrusts, from arrows and the like. Just so, our spiritual breastplate of righteousness protects us when we are slandered. It keeps us from being discredited in battle by wicked personal habits. There is very little better to protect you, my children, than an obedient life.

Shoes Of Peace

Next we come to the shoes. Very important, these shoes. An army moves on its feet.

Roman legionnaires' shoes are leather, able to be bound on tightly. And the soles are studded so a warrior won't lose his footing.

In my letter to you I call shoes the foundation of peace. Sweet Jesus! Praise you for your all-embracing peace, even in this place!

Let me be very honest with you. Prison has been no picnic. The food is moldy. Most of my companions have left me for easier places. I'm broke. There's running water though — down all four walls! And Nero is the emperor!

Should I worry? Should I tremble in fear? Why, let Caesar do his worst and God will do his best.

I learned from Jesus' death by crucifixion that God is the resurrection and the life. From then on I say, "Don't sweat the little things." And because of God everything is a little thing! So be at peace. God is sovereign. God is in his heaven and all is being watched over, cared for, loved, and held accountable.

Cornelius tells me there is great fear and confusion in battle. Soldiers hide in terror, they run, many even freeze up. And so it is in our spiritual warfare. Unless we have peace, we will not stand. We'll lose our footing and run.

Jesus said, "My peace give I unto you." Yes, let Caesar take my head, Jesus will but resurrect me to paradise!

Shield Of Faith

The fourth piece of battle gear a soldier takes on is his shield. It's made of wood glued together and covered with leather. Before a skirmish these would be soaked in water. This made them soft so they'd absorb much of the shock of a sword blow. And it also helped with darts.

The enemy learned to dip their arrows in pitch and light them with fire. Can you imagine 1,000 of these fiery darts raining down on an army? Why, soldiers would crouch behind their trusty shields and let the darts sink deep into its wet leather and be safely quenched.

So, too, Satan shoots his fiery darts at us. They are meant to burn and destroy. Darts of disappointment, of doubt, of fear, of rejection.

Why, only this morning I woke from a poor night's rest. And I had this sharp pain in my neck and arm. And suddenly the thought came burning into my mind — "Abandoned! No one cares about you. You're not loved. Your life is a waste. Even your own body hates you. The gospel is but a lying dream. There is no God! Paul, you're abandoned!"

For a moment I wallowed in such thinking. Then I realized it was one of Satan's fiery darts. And quickly I held up the shield of faith! As the prophet wrote, "When you pass through the waters they shall not overwhelm you. When you pass through fire you shall not be consumed. Fear not, I have called you by name." And I prayed, "Jesus, I know you. And I am persuaded that you are able to guard every day all I have entrusted to you."

Oh, my young Ephesian warriors for Christ, learn to use the shield of faith. It is your abiding trust in God that will allow you to quench every fiery dart of the devil.

The Helmet

Now for the helmet. Protecting the head is a necessity.

When I was a small boy, we'd play stick ball. And we were made to wear helmets so we wouldn't get hurt. I remember the first time the coach let me go in the game. I was so excited I ran in without my helmet and stick. The crowd roared with laughter.

I call this the helmet of salvation. (*Puts it on.*)

In life there is little of which I am certain — my health, my finances, if the Corinthian church is going to make it. But I am sure of this: That God loves me. That Jesus is my Savior. That I am his servant in the world.

69

Let me ask you: Are you a Christian? You hope so? You're trying to be? You're not sure?

Well, I'll ask you: Are you married? You hope so? You're trying to be? You're not certain?

Why, if a man is married, he knows it! There is proof — a ring, a memory, a wife, a public record. And it is no less with Jesus. We can be sure of our salvation. Jesus and I — we didn't get along together so well at first. I'd read his words, studied his life. And I was convinced it was all rubbish. But traveling to Damascus I met him and, falling off my horse, I lay at his feet asking life's two most important questions: Who are you, Lord? What will you have me do?

I didn't dream this up. I met him! I turned his way. I believe in him. I'm persuaded! I am sure in my head!

Sword

Now we come to the sword. So far all our battle armament has been defensive. Now we come to the first offensive tool of war — the sword.

Most soldiers of the day fight with long, heavy smiters, sharp on one side. It takes great strength to wield such a blade. Rome developed a shorter two-edged sword. One would come close to the enemy, grab him by the beard, and while he was trying to bring his sword up, use the short sword on his body.

You will notice the book of Revelation describes Jesus as having a tongue like a two-edged sword. At his temptation, Jesus told Satan repeatedly, "It is written." And he quoted scripture to rebuff him as if he were stabbing with a blade.

I tell you, the Word of God is living and active, sharper than any two-edged sword, piercing to the division of soul and spirit, of joints and marrow, and discerning the thoughts and intentions of the heart. And before him no creature is hidden, but all are open and laid bare to the eyes of him with whom we have to do.

With scripture we can stab the devil, route the wickedness of the day, slay injustice, and conquer every foe!

Prayer

Now we come to prayer, the invisible weapon. You will notice I mention it four times in my letter. I write, "Pray at all times in the Spirit with all prayer ..." "All prayer" means times in all its forms — praise, confession, gratitude, supplication, and intercession. "Pray at all times" — without ceasing.

What is there, young man, about "unceasing" you don't understand? A good soldier is in constant contact with his commander. Should we no less be in moment-by-moment contact with Jesus?

And notice it's pray "in the Spirit." We do not know how to pray as we ought. So the Spirit helps us in our weakness with sighs and groans too deep for words.

Be Alert

Next, there is a second unseen weapon one must put on — alertness.

Cornelius tells me his captain making the rounds one night found a sentry asleep at his post. Running him through with the sword, the commander simply said, "I found him asleep. I leave him asleep. Why should the entire army suffer for the negligence of one slacker?"

I remember how God pared Gideon's army down to 300. At the pool some soldiers stuck their faces in the water. They only wanted to quench their thirst, to fill their gut. Other soldiers, however, were vigilant. While on the lookout for the enemy, they cupped their hands and brought water to their lips. They became God's fighters.

My young friends, this world is no friend to the faith. Satan stalks around like a roaring lion seeking someone he may devour. You must be alert. You must watch over one another.

This brings me to the cleverest part of my comparison, something easy to miss.

You see, the best weapon of all is not the single soldier, but the entire army.

No soldier must fight alone. He'd be picked off by the enemy.

All of this battle gear is designed to be coordinated with other soldiers. Our shields lock together so we can advance as a wall.

When the enemy rains arrows down on us, our commander yells, "Turtlus," and we hold our shields over our heads making a protective roof. Like a turtle!

If one of us is hurt, we close ranks so there will be no gap.

My children, join God's army where you are. Don't wander off on your own. Don't keep running from this platoon to that platoon. You'll never find a perfect group of warriors. All soldiers have smelly socks! They're forever stepping on one another's feet.

No, I didn't mean it personally, Cornelius!

I asked one of my guards if the Celts that his army fought were very brave. "Aye," he said, "the Celts were very brave. We're just brave five minutes longer!"

My young friends, the evil day is upon us. You must put on God's armor and be brave just a little longer.

This is no time to be absent without leave, to be a malcontent, a deserter, or not to believe we can win.

It's time to enlist, to train, to suit up in God's armor. It's time to take a stand!

My, how I can get all worked up! But enough! Your young minds can only comprehend what your seats can endure. So you must get up and stretch, and go to your meals.

But first, a blessing! The grace of our Lord Jesus Christ, the love of God the Father, and the fellowship of the Holy Spirit be with you all. Amen!

Cornelius! Cornelius! My good man and guard, will you let these young warriors out so they can go to their posts and fight God's battles with him?

(*Lights dim.*)

Tenth Leper Speaks!

(*Levi ben Judah walks into the nave in a three-piece suit, wearing a fedora and carrying a leather briefcase. He stops, looks at the crowd, and intones ...*)

Yes, yes! Bless the Lord, oh my soul, and forget not all his benefits. (*Hesitates a moment and pulls out his pocketwatch, looks at the time, mumbles to himself.*) Oh my soul, how could I ever forget? How could anyone ever forget his benefits? (*This he says wonderingly while looking up. He sets his briefcase down on a table, opens it up, and extracts a business card. Offering it to no one in particular, he introduces himself, bowing.*) Levi ben Judah, son of Zion, husband to Martha, father of six, and might I add, cloth merchant extraordinaire! At your service!

Yes, I heard you'd been inquiring about me. Want to hear my story, I am told! Well, I'm here to provide!

It's in the Bible, you know. The physician Luke was careful to record it in some detail. Here, I'll read it to you. (*Says enthusiastically, then reaches for the book in his briefcase.*) Luke 17, verses 11 through 19 is the place.

"On the way to Jerusalem, Jesus was going through the region between Samaria and Galilee. As he entered a village, ten lepers approached him. Keeping their distance, they called out, saying, 'Jesus, master, have mercy on us!' When he saw them, he said to them, 'Go and show yourself to the priests.' And as they went, they were made clean. Then one of them, when he saw that he was healed, turned back, praising God with a loud voice. He prostrated himself at Jesus' feet and thanked him. Now he was a Samaritan. Then Jesus asked, 'Were not ten made clean? But the other nine, where are they? Was none of them found to return and give praise to God except this foreigner?' Then he said to him, 'Get up and go on your way; your faith has made you well.' "

Hey, that's me! He said that to me.

(*Puts down the Bible and says.*) It's like this.

I was born to a wealthy Samaritan family. We were textile manufacturers, dye experts, filled contracts for Caesar's army uniforms. Made a pile of money.

I liked my life. The right house, the right clothes, the right school, the right girlfriend. The right talent. My father said I was a born salesman, had the gift of gab, I did. Could talk myself out of a sunburn.

Dad turned the business over to me when I was 29. My wedding to Martha was the social event of the decade! The issue of our marriage was six children by the time I was 35. Ah, sweet prosperity. "Nothing can touch me now," I bragged.

I first noticed the itchy white patch on my hand ... here. (*Points then takes his coat off and rolls up his sleeve.*) It crept up my arm so quickly. Then it was on my neck, my face, in my scalp. At first when it was just a white scaly patch on my hand, I hid it from my wife. A tiny bandage just below my sleeve. Surely it is nothing. It will go away in a fortnight.

But as it spread, I began to fear the worst. I showed myself to a doctor and he pronounced the dreaded words. "Leprosy. Highly contagious. Incurable. Quarantine."

I couldn't even go home lest I infect my wife and my children. Village deputies fetched me a blanket, a water bottle, and told me to keep my distance, pointing me to a leper colony in the hills southeast of town.

"Please tell my wife," I pleaded. "She won't know what happened to me. Tell Martha I'm going over."

That first evening I entered the leper colony to find seven men and two women huddled intently around a pot, boiling their day's scavenging yield for a common meal. When I called out, hardly anyone looked up. "Another one," was all someone mumbled.

That first night as I lay on the ground under my blanket, my stomach rumbling after such a meager course of food, I rolled my head, looking around me in the firelight. Bandaged outcasts whose names I did not know snored in their sleep, moaned in some bottomless pain. And, oh! God, the stench.

I wept long into the night, my teeth clenched to stifle the sobs. "I'm a leper," I said to myself in disbelief. "In one day I've lost all — wife, children, job, society, health! All gone ... gone ... like golden leaves in autumn, I am a tree stripped bare of comforts. "Oh, God," I sobbed. "Why? Why me? What have I done to offend thee? Are you there? Do you care?"

(*Pauses.*) "Fifty yards," they instructed me. "No closer! It's the law."

Have you ever had to walk out to see your wife, tell her you're sick, a leper, contagious, incurable? And you're not coming home? And the closest you can get to her is fifty yards.

I could see her mouth drop open, her empty arms reach out to me; see her eyes well up, as she turned to flee the horror. Her wails haunted my sleep. I tell you, if hell had a sound, it sounded like this!

Five years. That's how long I lived in the colony. Zedekiah was the longest resident at seventeen years. A creek watered our camp. We scavenged for roots and fruit from trees. My wife came three times a week leaving supplies — bread, cheese, wine, meat. Seeing her at a distance, bearing gifts, was the only proof I wasn't in hell.

The ten of us were a colorful group. Zed was 63. Mary was only seventeen. I was a Samaritan. Two were from Judah. The rest were from Galilee. Joseph sang to entertain us. Salome was the best cook. Some had lost fingers, others noses, ears, or toes. We sat around the campfire and groused that if you put all our healthy body parts together, you'd only be able to make one decent human being.

Rainy nights were the worst. We kept to ourselves, alone with our thoughts of how much we'd each lost.

(*Pauses.*)

It was in the springtime that Martha made one of her visits. She yelled to me, her voice shrill, something about a man called Jesus. I couldn't make much out at a distance. So she shouted, "Read the note!" Gathering up the bundle, I found her letter. In it she told of a new rabbi in Galilee who would heal the sick, give sight to the blind. "Maybe this is the answer to my prayers," Martha wrote.

For weeks we discussed it. Was God real? Can anyone heal? Each of us in his or her own way begged the Almighty to visit such healing among us.

Then came the day like no other. We heard the singing, the jingle of tambourines. A festive parade along the road. A wedding? "No," a dancer shouted, "it is Jesus of Nazareth!"

The ten of us were on our feet, raggedly hobbling toward the crowd. Our hoarse voices chorused in one unrehearsed plea, "Jesus! Master! Have mercy upon us!" Some spat at us; others hissed and threw stones.

But Jesus stopped, fixed his gaze on us each, and spoke calmly, "Go, show yourselves to the priests!" His words were like a warm flower-scented breeze of summer. We turned, hesitant, afraid to hope, and began to collect our bearings. To the priest. In which village? We were bewildered. It had been so long since any of us had been anywhere. But suddenly, like a flock of crows, we became as one and began to move together as if in the thrall of an irresistible wind!

First Revi dropped his crutch, and I was curious. He went on without it. In our haste and bustle, our ragged bandages began to fall off. It's like we were unraveling. But when Mary dropped her veil and I saw her face ... beautiful ... I knew. I knew. I stopped still in my pell-mell dash. I began to rip at my clothes until I could see my arms, my chest — all clean! Like the flesh God once made me to be! Healthy!

There were sobs of joy, cries of utter disbelief! "Home! I'm going home!" someone shouted.

And then I saw Martha by the road in the shade of the tree. She was crying, holding those arms out to me. We rushed together in amazed passion. All I could keep saying is, "Can it be? Is the nightmare over? Am I really well?"

By now the rest of the ten were gone over the hill out of sight. And my Martha took my face in her hands and said, "Come home. There is so much catching up to do!" And we began to walk. Oh blessed day! I'm healed!

That's when it hit me. I'm not just lucky. No coin of mine, no learning or social connection had cured me. The man Jesus healed me.

"Martha," I said, "we must go and thank Jesus." And we did, falling at his feet, enthusiasms of thanksgiving pouring forth.

And that's when Jesus fixed his eyes upon me. They were eyes of such kindness. And he spoke. He spoke with sadness. He looked around and spoke, "Were not ten cleansed? Where are the other nine? Was no one found to give God praise except this foreigner?" Then he lifted me to my feet and quietly soothed, "Go your way. Your faith has made you well."

So that's how I made it home after five years. Back with my Martha. Back with my children. Back in the cloth business.

Yes, I'm back. But I'm not the same. Before the leprosy I felt lucky. After I met Jesus and he cured me, I feel blessed. And every day the sun rises I return to give Jesus praise.

(*Looks at his watch and up at the crowd.*) It's almost time for our little chapel to meet. Want to come? You'd fit right in. There is Bartimaeus who used to be blind until Jesus restored his sight. Samuel is there, who used to have a withered hand ... until Jesus bid him stretch it out. And Mary's always there. She used to be a prostitute until Jesus called her away. Fact is, all of us used to be one thing or another until we met Jesus. I figure you each have one thing or another Jesus can fix for you. So, come on along with me if you like. Sooner or later you'll get over feeling lucky. And you'll give thanks to God.

(*Levi ben Judah exits.*)